"C" THE CHRISTIAN JOURNEY

A 21-Day Devotional to Assist You in Your Christian Journey

By Erica McGraw

The Christian Journey
A 21-Day Devotional to Assist You
in Your Christian Journey
Second Edition

Copyright © 2020, Erica McGraw.
Contact the Author via e-mail at KingdomNews16@gmail.com.

All rights reserved. No part of this book may be reproduced, stored in a retrieved system, or transmitted in any form or any means, electronic, mechanical, photocopying, recording, scanning, or otherwise, without the prior written permission of the author.

Author: Erica McGraw
Editor: Anjeanette Alexander
Publication Services: Kingdom News Publication Services, LLC.

DISCLAIMER
All the material contained in this book is provided for educational and informational purposes only. No responsibility can be taken for any results or outcomes resulting from the use of this material.

While every attempt has been made to provide information that is both accurate and effective, the author does not assume any responsibility for the accuracy or use/misuse of this information.

Printed in the United States of America.
ISBN 978-1735362052

KINGDOM NEWS TODAY
Publication Services, LLC

Acknowledgements

I want to thank Christ Jesus for giving me this assignment to complete. In order to write about each topic discussed in the book, I had to face and deal with it in my own life, so I thank you, Lord, for Your grace and mercy in seeing me through this process. I am forever thankful for Your presence in my life.

I want to thank my mom, Nancy McGraw, for giving me a lifetime of love, support and encouragement. You have heard me say that as I was going through the process of accepting Christ in my life, I tried to hide it from you because of the trouble I gave you as a child about going to church. I'm thankful that I got to the point where I couldn't conceal it any longer; had I done so; this book may have never been written.

I want to give special thanks to my friend Duane Marshall and his lovely wife, Lisa. Duane, thank you for allowing the light of Jesus to shine through you and causing me to come to want what you had -- Him! I thank you both for your years of support. I will always love you.

In 2007, while I was participating in a support group, Dr. Barbara Cole said to me, "Wow Erica, you should write a book." Thank you, Sister Barbara, for dropping that seed. It has grown and been birthed. I am thankful to you and Brother Bryan. You were my Minnesota family, taking me in many times while I was there and away from my mom.

I also thank each and every person who has crossed my path and offered me any type of encouragement and/or push. There may have been times where I pushed back in a not-so-loving way, but now I realize the purpose behind those pushes and I am thankful.

God has so much in store for His people. I pray that each of you pushes forward to achieve all that God has for you. There is more than enough available to each of us. Be blessed in Jesus' Name!

This is the second edition of The Christian Journey. In the original edition one of the chapter names was changed, but it the edits never settled well with me, so I switched it out in this edition to reflect the original feelings I was personally experiencing. I know that what I was experiencing wasn't confusion, but I was in an in-between place that I described as being complacent. So, in this second edition, the chapter that was in the first edition titled Confusion is now a re-edit of the original titled Complacency.

Unless stated otherwise, all Scripture is from the King James Version of the Holy Bible.

Foreword

It is with great delight that I write this foreword, recognizing this labor of love from the heart of a giving, sensitive, and very determined woman of God who overcame the obstacles of life through her personal relationship with Jesus Christ.

As a pastor and friend, I know that Erica is well acquainted with more than her fair share of conflict and heartbreak. I am continually amazed by her spiritual strength and personal resilience in rising up — again and again — from the spiritual attacks and dark storms of life, and finding breakthroughs to the bright and ascended levels of restoration and achievement. *The "C"hristian Journey* is really her life's testimony of struggling and healing. It will bless those wounded by family, unfairly treated at work, or suffering from "church-hurt." It will cause all readers to thank God that we can be refreshed and renewed by His mercy and grace!

In these pages, Erica inspires us to find freedom from the attitude of defeat and anger to become all God has predestined us to become. We need not passively accept a victim's mentality when confronted by an accuser. God, as the author and finisher of our faith, has re-created us in Christ Jesus for victory: *"For we are His workmanship [His own master work, a work of art], recreated in Christ Jesus [reborn from above —*

spiritually transformed, renewed, ready to be used] for good works, which God prepared [for us] beforehand [taking paths which He set], so that we would walk in them [living the good life which He prearranged and made ready for us]" (Ephesians 2:10, Amplified Bible).

Erica shows us in this devotional that God will help us through our own passion and pain to heal our hearts and transform our lives. *The "C"hristian Journey* ministers to us ... it challenges us to be courageous, to be changed for the better!

Duane Marshall, Pastor
Love Changes Everything Ministries
Aurora, Colorado

Introduction

The purpose of this 21-Day prayer journal and devotional is to help you in your Christian journey. A form of healing takes place when you are able to write down and release inward thoughts and feelings that are not of God and that try to hold you back.

We know in John 10:10 that Satan is like a thief that comes to steal, kill and destroy. He often uses his same old tactics. His *main* tactic is tormenting our minds and planting toxic thoughts and feelings. When you hold those in, Satan is holding you captive.

But we also know, via that same passage of John, that Jesus came so that we might have life, and have it more abundantly! When we release what Satan planted in us, he can no longer use them against us because they have now been exposed. Satan is a master deceiver, but we are children of the Most High King, God Himself. When we received salvation, we were translated from the kingdom of darkness into the Kingdom of His dear Son (Colossians 1:13). The Kingdom of the Son is the Kingdom of Light. Darkness no longer has rule and reign because the light illuminates that which is dark and has dominion over darkness. We as Christians also have dominion, that is, the power to rule over all that is not of God.

Another key purpose of this 21-Day prayer journal and devotional is to help activate some things in your life. Statistics have shown that the ability to retain knowledge by listening only is less than the ability to retain knowledge by both listening and writing. That ability is even greater when one is able to listen, write and *do*. A study done at the University of Texas **(Metcalf, 1997)** revealed that people only remember:

- 10 percent of what they read
- 20 percent of what they hear
- 30 percent of what they see
- 50 percent of what they see and hear
- 70 percent of what they say
- 90 percent of what they do and say.

The study showed that reading, hearing, and seeing are passive traits. A passive person allows things to happen or accepts what others say and do without trying to change anything. As these attributes are utilized in conjunction with one another, the percentage of retention increases. But the study also revealed that once people begin to *speak* and *do* those things they see and hear, they move from a *passive* state to an *active* state. The word "active" is defined as participating in an action or activity, or being involved and participating. Once you move from being passive to being active, the things you do become a part of who you are instead of something you just read, see, or hear. James 1 speaks of being a *doer* of the word and not a hearer only. By turning the things, we read, hear, and see into constructive activities, we are able to better retain what God has in store for us.

It is God's desire that each of us lives a prosperous life. But God has a great enemy, and we must face that enemy as well. Once we decide to walk in the ways of the Lord and live a life that is pleasing to Him, we become an automatic enemy of the great deceiver, Satan himself. In Philippians 3, Paul speaks of suffering as Christ suffered. In verses 10-11, Paul says, *"That I may know him, and the power of his resurrection, and the fellowship of his sufferings, being made conformable unto his death; If by any means I might attain unto the resurrection of the dead."* Jesus was, and still is, the only human being to walk the earth and be without sin. Yet people lied about Him, beat and tortured Him, and ultimately crucified Him. In that day and age, the criminals were the ones being crucified; yet Jesus, who was without sin, was treated like a common criminal. He made the ultimate sacrifice. He knew what His purpose was when He came down from heaven ... to die for each and every one of us.

As Christians, we must be strong. Some of the topics in this devotional book will expose characteristics that may makes us appear weak. But through the Word of God, we can walk in the strength and power needed to survive during this journey. One thing to remember: We will all have moments of weakness from time to time. When you experience these moments, it does not mean you are a failure or that God doesn't love you; nor does it mean you're no longer saved. In Romans 3:23, we are told, *"for all have sinned, and come short of the glory of God."* God already knows this; He already knows we are not in accordance with His original plan for us. But know that God has every one of our weaknesses, flaws, gifts, and strengths already calculated into His divine plan for our lives!

We are not called to be perfect. We are called to be obedient to God's will and fulfill God's purpose for our lives. God referred to David as the man after His own heart; however, David was an adulterer and murderer with many other flaws. God knew David's heart, just like He knows the heart of each and everyone of us. So, if we believe in God's Word, confess our sins, and repent, we begin the road to restoration of His Glory in us.

I said earlier that we become Satan's enemy when we decide to follow the ways of the Lord. We need to remember not to join forces with the enemy and bring shame and condemnation upon ourselves out of guilt, hurt, or misunderstanding. The saying goes that we are our own worst enemies, but with God in the mix of all we do, we can believe the best in ourselves – because He is there *with* us.

God has shown me the importance of understanding what He is trying to impart to us so that we, His people, can be productive in advancing His Kingdom. That is, after all, why we are here. God created us to assist Him in building, developing and working within His Kingdom while giving Him glory.

Thus, it is my sincere prayer that something in this compilation of words given to me by the Lord will help you with your Christian journey. Here you will find many great and positive revelations, along with a few that may sting a little. This book is designed for the growth and development of your inner man so that you will be able to withstand the wiles of the enemy.

Table of Contents

CONFESSION 1

CONFIDENCE 6

CONVERSION 11

CYCLES 15

COPIOUS 19

COERCION 23

COMPASSION 27

COURAGE 34

CONFIRMATION 38

CHARACTER 42

COMPROMISE 47

CULTIVATION 53

CORRECTION 58

COMMITMENT 64

CLUTTER/CHATTER 70
CAPTIVITY 78
CONVICTION 86
CHALLENGES/CRITICISM 90
CALLING 99
COMPLACENCY 106
CHRIST JESUS 114
MESSAGE FROM THE AUTHOR 119
BIBLIOGRAPHY 121

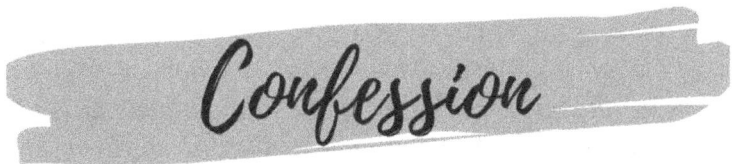

Confession

Confession is, first and foremost, the passage to our salvation. Romans 10:9-10 says, *"That if thou shalt confess with thy mouth the Lord Jesus, and shalt believe in thine heart that God hath raised him from the dead, thou shalt be saved. For with the heart man believeth unto righteousness; and with the mouth confession is made unto salvation."* Jesus died for us and to receive Him in our lives just requires us to confess our belief in Him and the work He did on our behalf. Once you confess His work, keep Him close, you will never go wrong trusting in Jesus.

When we first repent as sinners and accept Christ, *all* our sins, past, present, and future are immediately forgiven (Acts 10:43). Our spirit man is saved from *sin*, but are still subject to commit *sins*. Once we come to Christ, we confess those sins (1 John 1:9). Confessing is part of the conversion and sanctification process that helps Christians in dealing with sin and healing from it.

With confession comes reward. When you confess your sins *to* God, you are no longer bound by the things that try to hold you back from the things *of* God. We have all done things in our lives with which we are not happy or pleased. As our relationship with God grows, we come to a point where we can no longer hold those things inside.

God wants us to be free. He has given that freedom to us through His Son, Jesus. Romans 8:1-4 tells us, *"There is therefore now no condemnation to them which are in Christ Jesus, who walk not after the flesh, but after the Spirit. For the law of the Spirit of life in Christ Jesus hath made me free from the law of sin and death. For what the law could not do, in that it was weak through the flesh, God sending his own Son in the likeness of sinful flesh, and for sin, condemned sin in the flesh: That the righteousness of the law might be fulfilled in us, who walk not after the flesh, but after the Spirit."* In this Scripture, we are told that we no longer have condemnation because of Christ Jesus. We have been made free, so we should confess those things that would otherwise keep us bound.

Christians practice *humility* before God by confessing their sins to Him. It takes a humble person to admit his mistakes! Humility is a vital part of confession; it aids the restoration of Christians who have separated themselves from God by doing things that are not of Him. (God, in His Holiness, can't tolerate sin. So, sin is a wedge between us and Him.) The Apostle Peter says to "**Humble yourselves therefore under the mighty hand of God, that he may exalt you in due time**" (1 Peter 5:6). The Apostle John tells us that *"If we confess our sins, he is faithful and just to forgive us our sins, and to cleanse us from all unrighteousness"* (1 John 1:9).

We are to also confess our sins to one another as members of the body so that we can lift and strengthen each other via prayer. James 5:16 says, *"Confess your faults one to another, and pray one for another, that ye may be healed. The effectual fervent prayer of a righteous man availeth much."* And as confession to the Lord brings His forgiveness and deliverance, we are encouraged to share these scenarios as *testimonies* to glorify

God and encourage others. We testify about the life of sin we left and the freedom we experienced when we accepted Jesus Christ into our lives. We testify of experiences in which we as believers stumble, confess our sins, and are forgiven. With our testimonies, we whip the devil — Revelation 12:11 reads, *"And they overcame him by the blood of the Lamb, and by the word of their testimony ..."* There is deliverance in sharing your testimony; you keep the devil from using your past as a tool to keep you bound. There is healing in sharing those things that once brought you shame. A word of advice: Be mindful of where you share your testimony as well as who you share it with. Not everyone in your life will celebrate your spiritual advancement or your candor. As you begin to venture out, share where God leads you to share.

In confessing your sins, you must have a heart of repentance. That doesn't mean having a pity party for your past actions; it means that you stop an action once it is confessed so that you can move forward with what the Lord has in store for you. With an attitude of repentance, you humble yourself under the mighty hand of God so that at the proper time He may elevate you to fulfill purpose in your life.

All things happen for a reason, so don't be discouraged by your past. Confess and change those habits that are not Godly and *"press toward the mark for the prize of the high calling of God in Christ Jesus"* (Philippians 3:14). There is a lesson to be learned in every situation, so instead of being discouraged, ask the Lord what lesson He intended you to learn, and embrace it in order to have His will magnified in your life.

Confessing your sins is a way of giving thanks to God. You are thanking Him for your eyes being opened to the sin that you committed, and thanking Him for a newness of spirit. It's a way of thanking God for His presence in your life! Paul had his Damascus road experience. Beforehand, he hated Christians and did all he could do to persecute them. After his experience with the Master, he fell in love with the Lord Jesus Christ. The Spirit sent Paul on missions to share Christ with the Jews who were once like him ... and with the Gentiles. Paul, in his conversion, gained a passion for Christ and His people. Paul's mission was no longer the same; it was the complete opposite of what it had been previously. It was through his experience that he was able to confess his sins and adapt to a new focus in life. Paul, a powerful man in the Bible and the author of much of the New Testament, received wonderful lifesaving revelation from which we are still reaping the benefits today.

A spirit of humility will break down any strongholds of pride in our lives. By identifying and confessing our sins, we are telling the devil that we are no longer bound to him — we are now joint heirs to God's Kingdom through our Lord and Savior Jesus Christ. We have a place waiting for us in heaven. We are telling the devil that we will no longer do things his way; rather we will do things the Lord's way. Confession is freedom to the mind, body, and soul!

Caution: Once you confess your sins, you are forgiven of them and required to let them go ... for good. God has forgiven you; be sure to forgive yourself. There will be times where you'll be tempted to tiptoe back and pick up that guilt. Keep your mind made up that no matter what, you will follow Jesus.

PRAYER OF CONFESSION

Lord, I thank You for Your Son Jesus, who died on the cross for me and Who died for every one of my sins. I thank You that through the confession of my belief in Your Son, I was saved and set free from all condemnation that was set up against me. Lord, I ask You to give me a humble heart and an attitude of repentance so that I can closely walk with You and do Your will. Please bring to my mind any sins of thought, word, deed and omission that threaten to separate me from

You, so that I can confess these sins and ask Your loving forgiveness. I declare that the power of Satan no longer has a hold on me and that I walk in the redemptive power God has given to me though His Son, Jesus. And it is in Jesus' Name I pray. Amen.

Confidence

Due to circumstances in my life, I have often gone through times of low self-esteem. I know I am not the only one. And I am of the full understanding and belief that one does not suffer something for their own sake; as they overcome, they are then released to help others who come across their path. One of the things that keeps me going is best exemplified by this saying: "You have to go through to become new!" Once you can identify the issue, you can then determine a solution and focus on the area about which you need to pray.

I enjoy being around people and love to have a great time. But there have been times I didn't feel the best about myself. After I received salvation, these bouts of low self-esteem became fewer. Episodes did pop up periodically; however, their duration became shorter. I believe that as one comes to really believe who they are in Christ and how important they are to the plan of God, these "down" times diminish.

One day on my way to work, I was talking to God about confidence. Suddenly, a light bulb went off in my head. It was as though I *heard* a voice say, "It is difficult for those who have low-self-esteem issues to truly walk in confidence. If one is not comfortable within one's own self, their levels of confidence will be challenged each time something arises."

I began to study self-esteem and depression and wondered whether someone who is saved could suffer from bouts of depression. As I studied, I began to see many in the Bible who struggled with this very thing.

One of the articles I read was titled, "Do Real Christians Get Depressed?" Written by Stephanie Husk at the website Crosswalk.com, it began with a question: "What do Job, David, Elijah, Jeremiah and the Apostle Paul have in common?" It went on to reveal that every one of these great men of the Bible had experienced some sadness or sorrow ... what we may call depression today. We know that each of these men had powerful assignments and played a significant role in the Christian journey, yet they suffered. Despite their bouts of sadness and sorrow, they continued in the assignments the Lord placed on them — as we shall also do.

Don't believe the enemy when he tries to tell you that you are a failure. Don't believe those around you who may not fully understand what's going on inside you and try to discount or discredit you and your feelings. They may look at you and decide that you're being emotional when you are actually in a state of confusion and need help. Their words may be pushing you away. But when man pushes you away, press into God. He is always there to comfort you. Keep your faith; all you need is faith the size of a mustard seed. Activate that faith and hold on to it like it is the only thing on this earth. As you press into God, that faith will grow and help you leap over mountains that once seemed too big to conquer.

So, don't give up! Fight for Who you know your God to be. Remember, the fight isn't with man. The Word of God tells us that we wrestle not against flesh and blood, but against principalities. This is a spiritual fight. Just trust and believe that God is in the midst of it all ... and He will deliver you from all sorrow, all trouble, all calamity, all vexing spirits, all tormenting spirits, and every plan designed to keep you from the Almighty God.

Not only did those great men of the Bible suffer; our Lord and Savior Jesus Christ suffered. We see in Philippians 3:7-10 that it is an honor to suffer for the sake of Christ Jesus. Let's look at the Scripture.

> ***But what things were gain to me, those I counted loss for Christ. Yea doubtless, and I count all things but loss for the excellency of the knowledge of Christ Jesus my Lord: for whom I have suffered the loss of all things, and do count them but dung, that I may win Christ, and be found in him, not having mine own righteousness, which is of the law, but that which is through the faith of Christ, the righteousness which is of God by faith: That I may know him, and the power of his resurrection, and the fellowship of his sufferings, being made conformable unto his death; If by any means I might attain unto the resurrection of the dead.***

Until you really believe in your heart and mind that there is a purpose and a reason for everything that happens in your life, trials and tribulations will get the better of you. As you go through these trials that you don't understand, seek the Lord. As you grow in God, your confidence will be strengthened and the heaviness will dissipate. When sadness and sorrow try to enter your life, you will still be able to maintain peace and joy. It will reside in the innermost depths of your soul, and you will know that God will handle whatever *temporary* situation you may be going through. See, everything we face here on earth is temporary. We have power and authority to speak things into existence. So, once you begin to feel a certain way, you can decide to not allow that seed to take root.

Know that there are some things you must endure in order for you to be strengthened. In Psalm 30:5, we are told that *"weeping may endure for a night, but joy cometh in the morning."* You need to have confidence in God even when it seems hopeless and know that He is in the mix. He will never allow you to take on something He knows you cannot handle. He is the one Who created you, so He knows exactly what you can handle. He knows exactly what it will take to get you where He desires you to be. He has given us our own will, but it is His desire that we make a conscious decision to have His will rule and reign in our lives.

In Proverbs 3:5-6, it says, *"Trust in the LORD with all thine heart; and lean not unto thine own understanding. In all thy ways acknowledge him, and he shall direct thy paths."* God is right by our side; He is right there to direct our steps. But there is something we must do: acknowledge Him, trust Him, and walk in the confidence that He will direct our path at every turn and through every circumstance.

PRAYER OF CONFIDENCE

Lord, today I thank You for who You created me to be. I thank You for allowing me to live and breathe, and it is my desire that Your will for my life be manifested. Lord, today I ask that You give me the confidence to see You in every situation. I ask for confidence that will withstand the wiles of the enemy, who tries to break me down and keep me from You. I pray that no matter what is going on around me, I keep Your Word within my heart and I activate that Word to move mountains in my life.

Lord, there are days when the world feels like it is resting on my shoulders, and depression comes to bring me down. Let me stand tall, let me be immovable, let me stand with confidence that no matter what is happening around me or even to me, I shall prevail. I decree and declare that I shall not bend to the situation, but the situation shall bend and bow to the power and that authority that You have given to me. In Jesus' Name I pray, Amen.

Conversion

We are all triune beings and it is our spirit that is renewed at salvation. But our soul and body must be retrained to align with the reborn spirit received. It may take years to undo the hurt and pain that you endured prior to the experience of receiving Christ, but it can be done. As you move forward in the kingdom of God, adversity will come to hinder your progression. God knows this because of the trials and tribulations His Son endured while in the earth realm. Jesus was One who lived without sin in His life, yet He had to endure many hardships and take on the sins of the world. We are not exempt from hardship, but we can use the experiences of Jesus, and the ways in which He dealt with adversity, and apply them to our own lives. There is nothing so great that we cannot overcome it.

We need to know that it isn't always the devil that holds us back; sometimes it's our own inability to forgive and walk in God's divine unconditional love. As soon as we are able to give up self and take up the cross of Jesus, we will begin to see things turn around … and we will be able to walk in God's ways and according to His divine plan for our life. There must be a conversion that takes place, a conversion that will redirect our thoughts and past situations and point us in the direction of Christ. Christ walked this earth and served as our example. But until we can get out of ourselves and our own hurt feelings, we can't fully engage in the benefits He provided for us.

The transformation of a caterpillar into a butterfly is referred to as a metamorphosis. Once the caterpillar become a butterfly, it is converted. Its whole perspective is changed. It is unable to go back to what it once was. Allow me to back up a little and go into detail about the process that takes place during metamorphosis.

There are four stages in the life cycle of a butterfly. First, it's an egg. Once the caterpillar hatches, it eats a lot. It may eat one to two times its own weight in leaves each day. Thus, it outgrows its own skin and sheds it four to five times during this second stage of life. Then comes the third stage, where the caterpillar rests and transformation takes place. The word metamorphosis means to change form. Depending on the type of butterfly it will become, the caterpillar may burrow into the ground, hide behind loose bark or hollow logs, or rest in a silken cocoon that is spun from threads from its mouth. When spun into its cocoon, the caterpillar's body begins to change ... it liquefies. This is done because enzymes are being released that digest the caterpillar's tissue and convert into a rich medium. There are little cells inside that caterpillar called imaginal disks; as these are redeveloped, they become the wing structure and other integral parts of the butterfly. During the caterpillar's time in the cocoon, its muscles and entire digestive system have now changed from their former state, along with its heart and nervous system. The entire system is rebuilt. In the final stage, a beautiful butterfly struggles out of the cocoon. If there is human intervention during this time of struggle, the butterfly can become crippled and not make it. The struggle it must endure during this conversion is what makes the butterfly strong.

The act of being converted into a member of the Kingdom of God is as simple as saying yes. But the process of walking that process out, and *living* that membership, is where the learning curve needs to be applied. You will need to learn to leave old mindsets behind and walk in the newness of what the Lord has done for you. You can no longer walk in the ways of the world. There are some who try to carry their worldly ways over into the Kingdom, and that just will not work. If you were a "con" in the world, you cannot be a con in the Kingdom. Those who operate in the Spirit will be able to discern where you are coming from. But that doesn't even really matter — God knows all things. Allow the conversion to change your mindset. Increase your trust in the Lord and allow Him to direct your path. Paul experienced his Damascus road experience, and when he came out of that situation he was completely converted, just like the butterfly. Paul was not turning back. He once persecuted those who followed Christ. After his transformation, he walked with the same convictions ... but for the good instead of for the bad.

As mentioned earlier, we are triune beings who must submit to the will of God, allowing Him to mold and shape us. Our spirits are renewed when we accept His Son, but our bodies and souls need to come in alignment. We allow our struggles to make us stronger. It is during these times that you need to *concentrate* on what God is speaking to you and walk in *obedience* to Him. He will direct your steps and tell you what you need to do. He will comfort you, He will console you, and He will give you peace and joy. Don't ever give up! Let me repeat that — don't ever give up! There will be times you feel like throwing in the towel, but you can't. There is a purpose for the struggle, just as there is a purpose for everything that comes our way. The Lord said He will never leave us nor forsake us. He knows all and sees all, so He will not allow more to come your way then you can handle. So, when trials come, learn to trust Him. It saddens His heart when His people try on their own power to do what

He has promised to do for them. We aren't meant to use our own power and strength to deal with our problems. That is why, when Jesus left earth, He said He would send a Comforter — the Holy Spirit.

See, just as we are triune beings, so is God. But I am sure you already knew that since the Word says we were created in His image. Embrace everything that God has for you and allow God to shape and mold you into the person He desires you to be.

PRAYER OF CONVERSION

Lord, I yield to You and ask that You transform me into the person You want me to be. Allow my mind, body and soul to come under Your leadership and Your ways. I ask that, as this transformation takes place in my life, I do not look back and wish to retain anything from my old life, but rather look forward to the new things You have in store for me – a new vision, new experiences, a solid foundation in You and a deep trust in You and Your ways. Don't let me waver; let me be steadfast in seeking You at all times for all things. Allow me to have a spirit of gratitude for Your presence in my life, and walk in the newness You have given me. In Jesus' Name I pray, Amen.

Cycles

Have you ever seen the movie *Groundhog Day*? In this movie, the character, played by actor Bill Murray, kept waking up and repeating the same day as though it had not even happened before. The same thing can happen in the spirit realm to Christians if they do not follow the Word of God. In order for cycles in our lives to be broken, we need to have a spiritual awakening. We need to be rooted in God's Word. We need to come to a place of allowing our spirits to be enlightened rather than falling back to sleep and into the same old patterns, preventing the Word from taking root so that deliverance can be achieved.

It's not always the enemy causing our problems. It may be our own inability to walk in God's divine, unconditional love. Oftentimes we expect to *receive* unconditional love, but are not ready to *give* it. That creates an imbalance and causes our lives to spin out of control like malfunctioning revolving doors. As soon as we are able to give up self and take up the cross of Jesus, the cycles will be broken ... chain will be broken ... and strongholds and generational curses removed, making way for change to come into our lives.

We need to understand that some of the cycles we face involve things that occurred before we even entered this earth realm officially. We could be battling issues first battled by our grandparents or parents; these are often referred to as generational curses. We have no control over what happened in the past with them, but we do have a say as to how these issues will affect us and the generations to come. Once you identify what hinders you, you will be able to move forward in conquering it. We are told in Romans 8:37 that *"we are more than conquerors through him that loved us."* We are truly loved by God. He created us and He has a purpose for us. But, again, He also has an adversary. That adversary will do anything to keep us from walking in our rightful place.

To overcome these cycles, we must evaluate ourselves. We need to go in deep and find the root of all things that are keeping us from walking in the fullness of God's glory. One such root may be a deep-seated root of rejection — when you feel you aren't accepted, you retreat into areas of spiritual darkness, believing the lies of the enemy.

The hindering spirits that keep us separated from God's best don't come alone; they like to stick together and work as a tag team. I remember the Lord showing me once how these spirits are like a big ball of tape. As one spirit comes and attaches itself to you, it brings others — and they try to throw a party! You may start out with a spirit of rejection, but with that come feelings of abandonment, judgment, pride. And before you know it, you are a big, dark, heavy ball of emotional mess. People around you will see these spirits and try to categorize you. They will try to make you feel that you are just *pretending* to be saved. You may reach out for help, only to find that the people you thought you could turn to are the ones who turn their backs to you.

It's all a part of Satan's plan. He wants to isolate you, infiltrate your mind, and get in your thoughts. Just remember your salvation in Christ according to Romans 10:9-10: "*If thou shalt confess with thy mouth the Lord Jesus, and shalt believe in thine heart that God hath raised him from the dead, thou shalt be saved. For with the heart man believeth unto righteousness; and with the mouth confession is made unto salvation.*" Jesus knows how valuable you are to His Father's Kingdom, so He chose to come to earth, be the sacrificial lamb, and go to hell so He could defeat the devil, return to earth and ascend to heaven, where He is now seated at the right hand of the Father. And He sent the Comforter, the Holy Spirit, to reside in you and empower you. In 1 John 4:4, we are told that "*greater is he that is in me then he that is in the world.*" The Holy Spirit is the third person in the triune being of God and, therefore, is the very essence of God the Father. The Holy Spirit will comfort you in times of darkness; no matter how lonely you may feel, He is there for you. He will speak to you. He will show you your errors and put you in the right direction.

During your time of self-evaluation, you may have to go all the way to the foundation. You may have built your life on certain beliefs and understandings, only to realize there are cracks in your foundation. As you are walking on a sidewalk, you may see a big crack caused by a tree root that grew under that sidewalk and had caused the concrete to shift. Repairing the sidewalk may involve digging up and removing the root to level out the sidewalk's foundation. Maybe your foundation was built on unstable ground, and an excavation needs to be done to ensure that the ground is secure the next time you build. In Matthew 7:24-27, we are told to build our house on the rock so that when the storms come, the house will remain. Storms come into our lives all the time and if we don't have a solid foundation, we are like a foolish man who builds his house on sand. God desires us to be victorious over every storm. That victory is possible ... we just need to decrease ourselves, our thoughts, our ways and submit to His ways. God is always on our side and through Him, our unhealthy cycles can be broken. Press into God and allow Him to direct your steps. He will make your crooked paths straight.

Know that you are an overcomer and that nothing in this world can keep you down. God is on your side at all times, and His angels are available to you. He will dispatch those angels to assist and protect you in times of trouble. Don't forget — the Holy Spirit is available to reside in you. Remember, you are covered. Don't allow unhealthy cycles to stop what God has for you.

PRAYER FOR BREAKING CYCLES

I declare on this day that I will put my trust in God; I will allow Him to search my heart and reveal to me all those things the enemy thinks he has on me. I am walking in God's divine Power and Authority, and God's power is victorious over the power of the enemy. No weapon of the enemy shall hinder me. I declare that cycles of hurt, shame, rejection, abandonment, abuse, and any other harmful cycles will be broken in my life. I declare that every generational curse affecting my life shall be broken today. I put my trust and belief in God. Man may let me down, but I know in my heart that God will not. Lord, I thank You and I bless Your name. In Jesus' Name I pray, Amen.

Copious

The Lord sometimes speaks to me by dropping just one word in my spirit. Other times, He will drop a Scripture in my mind so that I will think about it and meditate on it. This particular time, He gave me a Scripture that had been resonating in my spirit for several weeks. And, on my way to work one day, He gave me the word *copious*. I love to learn, which is a good thing because oftentimes the words God gives me are words with which I'm unfamiliar. That means I am forced to look up that word and learn the meaning of it before I can really understand the reason God has given it to me. This particular day, I quickly did a Google search for *copious* to find out that it means "abundant in supply and quantity." Synonyms of this word include *full, extensive, generous, lavish, liberal, overflowing, numerous, many*, and *plenteous*. Immediately, the Scripture that had been in my spirit came to life for me in a whole other dimension.

The Scripture that has been resonating in my spirit was John 10:10: *"The thief cometh not, but for to steal, and to kill, and to destroy: I am come that they might have life, and that they might have it more abundantly."* We all know that the devil is the thief in this Scripture, but I have been focusing on the second part of the Scripture, where Jesus is telling us that His purpose for coming to earth was so that we could have life and have it more abundantly. He came so that we could have a *copious* life

— in other words a life that is overflowing, a life that is lavish due to His love, a life of more than enough. And it's a life that is available to anyone who desires to partake.

In this Scripture, Jesus is telling us, "Do not get discouraged or bogged down by the ongoing tricks and lies of the adversary. Turn to me for abundant life, sustaining life. No matter what your circumstance or situation is, you can still walk in joy, peace and love; that is why I came and why I am coming back again. Don't worry about your enemies; if you put your trust in me, you will not even be able to see them." In Psalm 23, we are told that He will prepare a table before us in the presence of our enemies. We are all going to have enemies, but we don't have to focus on them; we can focus on Christ and the abundance of what He has in store for us.

God also began to share with me about being obedient and about receiving blessings through giving. One evening I was sitting in Bible study, and the Lord spoke to me about giving a love offering to the speaker. Thinking about the amount of cash in my purse, I decided to give a percentage of it.

"Give it all," God said.

I began to go back and forth in my thoughts, trying to decide whether I should be obedient or whether I should give the amount I'd been planning to give. Just then, the speaker began to make some statements that let me know without a doubt that God was using this person to rebuke my thoughts right on the spot! I decided to obey God and give all that I had. If I hadn't listened to God, I could have stopped, or at least hindered, something He intended to do in my life. It was just a matter of putting my full trust in God. The awesome thing about it was that the next day when my sister brought the mail in, she told me, "You may want to look at the mail. It looks like there's a check in there." She was right! It was an unexpected check. I was looking at my supply — what I had in my wallet. God was telling me, "I am your supply. I have the abundance and I am the Source. I can open doors you know nothing of. But I require you to trust Me. I require you to be obedient. I require you to decrease *your* thoughts and desires and follow Me." When Jesus began His ministry, He told those He'd chosen to be His disciples to come and follow Him. It is never mentioned that anyone said no. It would seem that those chosen ones saw something different about Him and wanted to follow Him! Jesus walked in authority and in abundance. That copious nature was upon Him, and people were drawn to Him even before He began to do miracles.

Allow your life to be filled with the abundance that Jesus came to give you. Don't allow hindrances to keep you from walking in fullness and joy. Don't allow them to steal your happiness. Don't allow them to harden your heart and turn you into someone you can't even recognize in the mirror. Rise and take authority; rise and take dominion of your own life; rise and be the free and liberated being that Christ created you to be.

PRAYER TO FULFILL THE COPIOUSNESS OF GOD IN YOUR LIFE

Lord, I thank You for Your Son, who came so that I can live a copious life, a life that is filled with abundance; a life that has power and authority over lack; a life that is full of potential. I thank You for the abundance of love given me through Your dear Son, Jesus. I thank You that He is the Way, the Truth and the Life. I thank You that through Him I have been adopted into the kingdom of light and that I am redeemed by the blood of the Lamb. I thank You that no weapon formed against me shall prosper. Lord, I ask that Your ways become my ways and that my life be full of abundance — not just for me, but for those I encounter and am destined to help bring into Your Kingdom as well. Allow me to live a life pleasing to You in ALL that I do. In Jesus' Name I pray — Amen!

Coercion

There will be many times in your Christian journey that you will encounter people who are stuck in church "traditionalism." They will follow church rituals that have gone on longer than anyone can remember. They may pretend to be progressive or innovative. But as you observe their methods, you will find that underneath their veneer, they harbor a traditional point of view. Even worse, they think *you* should be traditional, too. Even when it comes to the way you worship God.

The Bible states that we are to worship God in spirit and in truth. Worship comes from within. One cannot be forced to worship if one is not willing. Sometimes, the atmosphere needs to be established and the presence of God needs to be ushered in for people to enter into a proper spirit of praise and worship. If a minister stands before a congregation and fusses about the people not responding according to how he thinks the people should respond during worship, it is almost intimidation. If people feel intimidated, they will not freely enter into worship.

I once heard a preacher say that praise has to be manufactured. Again, I am a stickler for learning the true meaning of a word ... especially when, as was this case, it's used in a way that causes something within me not to feel right. So, I decided to research the word "manufacture." I learned that it means to "make" or "produce" or "fabricate." The independent definition of "fabricate" means to invent or concoct something, typically with a deceitful intent; or to falsify or fake. I then began to ask, "How can one *manufacture* praise?" The Lord showed me that if we offer Him a fake or fabricated praise, we might as well not offer it at all. He said that our praise should be *authentic*, which means it should be pure and genuine. Our praise should come from who we truly are. We can't compromise our praise to fit the way man desires us to praise. We shouldn't let man coerce us into praising God a certain way by using force or threats or by pressuring us; none of it is pleasing to the Father if it is not authentic. We may all be bound together as Christians, but our personal journeys differ. Because they differ, my praise may not look like your praise. Just because we praise God differently does not mean God is not receiving His glory from one of us!

A woman, who also happened to be a minister, once teased me for the way I praised and worshipped God. Now I have a playful personality; I tease my friends and loved ones. But when this woman was teasing me, it was done in a demeaning manner, not a joking one. She was trying to intimidate me, trying to instill fear in me, trying to plant seeds to make me feel as though I was doing something incorrectly. She was being a church bully, misusing her authority. But I had my own relationship with God ... one strong enough for me to realize that I had to be obedient to *Him*. That is how we all have to be — determined to follow the ways of the Lord no matter what. When we bow down before Him and worship Him, we must do it in spirit and in truth.

Many people become set in their ways. They become complacent, defined by Oxford Dictionaries online as "showing a smug or uncritical satisfaction with one's self or one's achievements." They become resistant to change. This played out on my job when we got a new boss. When the new boss came in, it was discovered that many of the processes being followed were not up to policy. When updating of the old processes began, many of the employees who had been with the company for years kept saying, "But this is the way we have *always* done it." This is how some Christians are as well! They get in a comfort zone and have no desire to change their way of doing things. They are satisfied with the status quo and get anxious about stepping out into the deep. Remember Luke 5:1-6, where Jesus told Peter to cast his nets into deep water? Peter answered, "Master, we have toiled all the night, and have taken nothing: nevertheless, at thy word I will let down the net." (v. 5). It was Peter's obedience and willingness to try something new that allowed his nets to be filled with more than enough — so much so that the net broke. In fact, the amount of fish Peter caught threatened to sink his ship *and* that of his partners, whom he'd called for help.

See, we can't allow the thoughts and feelings of others to keep us from what God has for us. Nor should we allow ourselves to be held back by our own unwillingness to change. Each day we wake up is a new day to do wonderful things for the Lord.

I just want to encourage you to not let those stuck in customs and traditions or those with hatred in their hearts keep you from moving forward. Don't allow them to put your light out through coercion. It doesn't matter how long you have been saved; it doesn't matter how long they were there before you. God's nature changes not. But He does send fresh wind — and you may just be the fresh wind God sent! Be strong and confident in who God created you to be. People who are set in traditionalism are usually not willing to accept change, so your freshness ensures that there will be challenges that will hinder your advancement if you aren't walking in full confidence of who you are and what God is telling you to do. Adversity comes, but you can overcome it. Stay out of the flesh and walk in Jesus. Smile! God loves you and will mold you into who He wants you to be if you surrender to Him and remain obedient to His guidance.

PRAYER TO OVERCOME COERCION

Lord, I thank You that Your Spirit is available to me. I thank You that Your Spirit leads me and guides me. I thank You, Lord that You know my heart and that You have created me to praise and worship You in my own unique way. Lord, don't allow others to intimidate me into doing things the way they think I should do them. Strengthen me to follow Your leading and guiding. Give me a heart to worship You in spirit and in truth. In Jesus' Name I pray, Amen.

Compassion

Let us look at the word compassion. And let's look at a word with which it's sometimes confused: Passion.

The words compassion and passion are related, but different. *Compassion* is defined at Dictionary.com as "a feeling of deep sympathy and sorrow for another who is stricken by misfortune, accompanied by a strong desire to alleviate the suffering." If you are a *compassionate* person, you have empathy for, and a desire to help, those who are sick, hungry or in trouble. Compassion is an attribute we are clearly shown in the Word that, as followers of Christ, we should have because of our relationship with Him. Jesus showed compassion for others in numerous instances throughout the Gospels. Those acts of compassion are what we know as miracles ... healing the sick, giving sight to the blind, and even raising the dead.

In Matt. 25:31-46, Jesus tells the story of the sheep and the goats, and the thing that distinguishes the two groups.

> **When the Son of man shall come in his glory, and all the holy angels with him, then shall he sit upon the throne of his glory: And before him shall be gathered all nations: and he shall separate them**

one from another, as a shepherd divideth his sheep from the goats: And he shall set the sheep on his right hand, but the goats on the left. Then shall the King say unto them on his right hand, Come, ye blessed of my Father, inherit the kingdom prepared for you from the foundation of the world: For I was an hungred, and ye gave me meat: I was thirsty, and ye gave me drink: I was a stranger, and ye took me in: Naked, and ye clothed me: I was sick, and ye visited me: I was in prison, and ye came unto me. Then shall the righteous answer him, saying, Lord, when saw we thee an hungred, and fed thee? or thirsty, and gave thee drink? When saw we thee a stranger, and took thee in? or naked, and clothed thee? Or when saw we thee sick, or in prison, and came unto thee? And the King shall answer and say unto them, Verily I say unto you, Inasmuch as ye have done it unto one of the least of these my brethren, ye have done it unto me.

Then shall he say also unto them on the left hand, Depart from me, ye cursed, into everlasting fire, prepared for the devil and his angels: For I was an hungred, and ye gave me no meat: I was thirsty, and ye gave me no drink: I was a stranger, and ye took me not in: naked, and ye clothed me not: sick, and in prison, and ye visited me not. Then shall they also answer him, saying, Lord, when saw we thee an hungred, or athirst, or a stranger, or naked, or sick, or in prison, and did not minister unto thee? Then shall he answer them, saying, Verily I say unto you, Inasmuch as ye did it not to one of the least of these, ye did it not to me. And these shall go away into

everlasting punishment: but the righteous into life eternal.

As we develop as followers of Jesus, we will want to feed the hungry, clothe the naked, visit the sick and imprisoned. We will have trouble turning our backs to any kind of suffering.

Passion is defined as a "powerful or compelling feeling or emotion, as love or hate." Your compassion for those less fortunate than you can obviously run hand in hand with your passion for a mission that helps the unfortunate. When you are *passionate* about a mission, you become protective of it. You begin to invest not only your prayers into that mission; you invest your time, talent, and treasure into it. You become emotional about that mission, because you care about it so much. You have such a passion for it that when you see others disrespecting, badmouthing or abusing it, you may become hurt to the point of anger.

Sometimes passion can be mistaken for compassion. Let's say you have just given your life to Christ, and you look at your unsaved friends and have compassion for them due to their unfortunate (unsaved) condition. But your newfound passion for following Christ causes you to be overbearing and condemning. I can attest to this. When I first got saved, I was so excited about my newness of life that, as I was trying to share Christ with my best friend, I condemned her. At the time, I didn't realize what I was doing. But as I matured in the Lord, I realized that in my zeal and excitement — along with my desire for my friend to experience what I was experiencing — I ended up condemning her actions. As a result, our friendship slowly dissolved. It didn't happen immediately, but the phone calls and visits got fewer and fewer until we just went our separate ways. We didn't have a fight or a fall out; the relationship it just slowly faded. So, we must make sure our passion doesn't overpower and nullify our compassion.

Allow me to address emotions for a moment. I made mention earlier of us as triune beings – body, soul, and spirit. Emotions are housed in the soul. This is also where beliefs, attitudes, feelings, and memories are housed. In addition, the soul is the seat of the conscious mind, which includes our thinking and reasoning.

Let's look at this a little deeper. If you are *passionate* about something, you will begin to be sensitive to the things and the people that come against it. Your feelings and your belief systems will be challenged. It may seem as though everything is coming at you at one time. You may feel unequipped to handle it all, so your emotions begin to take control. Your thoughts begin to take over and your feelings/emotions also begin to overwhelm you. What is happening is that you are leaning on your own understanding — not fully trusting that God has it under control. This is a sign that more prayer is needed in your life. It is also a sign that you need to pull on Jesus just a little more because His fruits of the spirit aren't fully in operation in your life. Galatians 5:22-23 says, *"But the fruit of the Spirit is love, joy, peace, longsuffering, gentleness, goodness, faith, Meekness, temperance: against such there is no law."* These aren't just pleasant words we should live by; these are the characteristics of God. In these characteristics can be found compassion. Since we are made in God's image, they are also the fruits that should be evident in our lives. When your emotions overtake you, it's time to turn to the Father and allow Him to calibrate you. When He does, you will be able to show your *compassion* toward people without your *passion* for your mission getting the better of you.

Our passion can also lead to despair. Don't get overwhelmed and feel like a failure if you have struggled in the past or are struggling now. I completely love the story of Peter. Just before Jesus was arrested, He told Peter that before the cock crowed, he was going to deny Jesus three times. Peter was like, "No I won't." Peter was a close follower of Jesus. He witnessed many of the miracles Jesus had done; Jesus had even enabled him to walk on water! Peter had a divine revelation from God the Father; when Jesus asked in Matthew 16, "Who do men say that I am?" Peter answered, "You are the son of the living God." Jesus told him, "Flesh and blood did not reveal that to you, but the spirit of God did." Peter was one of the men chosen to go pray with Jesus. Peter reaped financially by obeying Jesus' order to go back out after he and his men had fished all night and received nothing. Peter was the one who cut off the ear of the man who was trying to take Jesus into custody. (This was an act of *passion* on Jesus' behalf; Jesus then showed *compassion* by immediately healing the man's ear.) Peter experienced a lot through his relationship with Jesus. But as Jesus predicted, Peter denied Jesus three times. After Peter realized what he had done, he felt awful. He probably felt that he'd betrayed the one who taught him.

The Roman soldiers took Jesus, beat him, and crucified him. Jesus told the disciples beforehand what was to come, but the chaos and their personal feelings must have caused them to forget about all the miracles. They must have forgotten that He brought Lazarus back from the dead after four days. They were mourning for Him, forgetting most of what He had spoken to them. But the day came when He rose from the dead. He revealed Himself to people, some of whom didn't even realize who He was. In Mark 16, when the women came to anoint Jesus' body, they found a young man in the tomb who told them to tell Jesus' disciples *and Peter* that Jesus has risen and gone into Galilee. Peter was singled out! Yes, Peter fell short in his devotion and denied Jesus. But God also knew what was planted within Peter and the purpose that Peter had to accomplish. Sometimes, we get to a place where we have to forget about our failures and focus on our future and our destiny. In Isaiah 64:6, the Bible says, *"But we are all as an unclean thing, and all our righteousnesses are as filthy rags; and we all do fade as a leaf; and our iniquities, like the wind, have taken us away."* Then in Romans 3:23-25, *"For all have sinned, and come short of the glory of God; Being justified freely by his grace through the redemption that is in Christ Jesus: Whom God hath set forth to be a propitiation through faith in his blood, to declare his righteousness for the remission of sins that are past, through the forbearance of God."* God knows we are human and that we will make mistakes. Because of His compassion for us, He gave us the blood of His Son to save us. Peter was forgiven and Jesus knew Peter had a great work to do, so He had to get to Peter and encourage Him to keep moving. His message to Peter, in today's language, was this — "Don't get stuck. You messed up, but it's time to get back on your feet and run this race."

When we fail, we tend to want to give up. But our failures should get us motivated to do better. Allow your failures to strengthen you, not tear you up. Keep your thoughts in check, because when you mess up that is a foothold for the enemy to enter and attempt to plant wicked thoughts for you to mull over. As Jesus told His disciples what was to become of Him, Peter jumped in and began to rebuke Him. But Jesus' response was, *"... Get thee behind me, Satan: thou art an offence unto me: for thou savourest not the things that be of God, but those that be of men."* (Matthew 16:21-23). Peter may have thought he was showing compassion for his teacher, but Jesus knew that His crucifixion was God's will. Since Peter was unconsciously speaking against the will of the Father, Jesus had to rebuke the one who prompted Peter's misguided compassion.

Don't give up when the going gets tough. Stay encouraged and know that God is in the midst of all things. Not some things, but ALL things. Nothing happens without God knowing about it or even allowing it to happen. He is a sovereign God, meaning He is the one Who exercises supreme authority. There is none higher than Him, so learn to trust Him and rely on Him for all things. Learn to love like Him and develop a relationship with Him. When He gives directions, follow them. Don't allow the ways of this world to hinder you from doing the things of God. Your life is eternal — strive to make it an eternal life in heaven with the Creator.

PRAYER FOR COMPASSION

Lord, I thank You for the compassion You have placed in my heart. As I continue to be compassionate, strengthen me with the confidence I need to stand firm in my belief that you are leading and guiding me. Help me to keep my passion from overtaking me and nullifying my compassion. Give me discernment to know when it is you leading and guiding me, and when I have gone astray and must change my focus back to You. The enemy will try to trick and deceive me, but as Your Word says, the voice of a stranger I will not follow. I stand on that Word and will trust You. Lord, I ask that as persecution comes for my stepping out in faith and showing compassion to others, I will not waver, but I will be confident in who You are in me. In Jesus Name I pray, Amen.

Courage

In the Bible are several Scriptural passages in which someone was admonished to be "of [a] good courage." Courage is mentioned in a number of Scriptures and clearly emerges as essential to a successful Christian walk.

You can't be cowardly and walking in courage. Cowardliness and courage are opposites ... and courage will take you so much further.

Perhaps the best-known passage that mentions courage is Joshua 1. In this chapter, we learn that Moses is dead; the responsibility for leading the children of Israel has been passed on to Joshua. Earlier, when twelve spies were sent to scope out the Promised Land for forty days, Joshua and Caleb were the only two who came back with a positive report. The other ten spies came back walking in fear and speaking doom, and Israel had to spend 40 years wandering in the wilderness.

To be courageous means to be bold, brave, fearless, gallant, unwavering, and firm in your decisions. When you begin to step out in new areas, fear will sometimes try to grip you and keep you immobile. But in order to walk with God, we must be willing to step into the unseen whenever God tells us to move. Faith and courage go hand in hand. Faith is stepping out on something that is unseen; courage is what is needed to take the step.

For an example, let's return to the story of Joshua. Just as the Lord had directed Moses, He directed Joshua by giving him instructions for leading the people safely, and after their time in the wilderness was up, taking them into the Promised Land. We read in Joshua 3 that the people reached the Jordan River at a time of year during which flooding was common; in fact, the river was already outside of its banks. Nevertheless, the Lord told Joshua to command the Levitical priests to carry the Ark of the Covenant a few steps into the river, then stop. Once they did so the waters parted, allowing all the children of Israel to pass through. Joshua had to have faith and courage to impart those instructions, while the priests had to have faith and courage to follow them. The same is the case with the 12 men, one from each tribe, chosen to select stones from the middle of the dry riverbed to construct a campsite memorial, again per God's instructions to Joshua.

Yet today, God will instruct you to do things that may seem downright scary. When it happens, be of good courage! Know that He will always lead and guide you in the right direction ... and He will never leave or forsake you.

A close relative of fear, and therefore an enemy of courage, is discouragement. Discouragement is defined by Oxford Dictionaries as "a loss of confidence or enthusiasm; dispiritedness."
When difficult circumstances arise, don't allow them to beat you down, no matter what the situation or how long it has persisted. There are many times I may get discouraged and questions flood my mind. There may even be times when I may say, "What's the use?" But then, I realize that the things I do aren't for man. I have to look beyond the situation and know the real reason I must carry on. I encourage you to do the same.

The assignment God has given you may look intimidating. You must keep your eyes on Him and draw your courage from Him.

As you carry out your assignment, you may find that people don't understand you, but you must trust God, not man. As a child of God, you are extremely valuable to Him. But different spirits will come and try to bring you down – especially the spirits of fear and discouragement. Your mind may begin to wander and you may begin to think things that are not the truth, not of God. That's when you have to fight! We are told in 2 Corinthians 10:3-5 that we have to guard our minds: *"For though we walk in the flesh, we do not war after the flesh: (For the weapons of our warfare are not carnal, but mighty through God to the pulling down of strong holds;) Casting down imaginations, and every high thing that exalteth itself against the knowledge of God, and bringing into captivity every thought to the obedience of Christ ..."* It is important that you cast down those vain imaginations as they come. You have that authority. Sometimes it's difficult, but it must be done. If you don't close the door for unhealthy spirits to invade your thoughts, you will begin to be controlled by them. It is then that Satan will try to convince you that he has you. But don't give up — be of good courage. Remember: Your redemption is in Christ Jesus. You are more than a conqueror through Him (Romans 8:37) and you can do all things through Christ who strengthens you. (Phil. 4:13).

And you are equipped with weapons to fight the devil's influences ... one of the most powerful being prayer. In 1 Thessalonians 5:17, we are told to *"pray without ceasing."* Prayer is something you can do at any time. Your prayers don't have to be loud or sound King James-y. Prayer is simply speaking to God. It's simply telling Him what's on your mind and in your heart. Prayer is a form of meditation during which you express yourself to God, but it's also a time during which God will reveal Himself to you. The neat thing is He already knows all, so most of the time He is just waiting on us to come to Him. (God is a gentleman and will never, ever impose His will on us. We have free will, but it is His desire that we seek for our will to align with His all-knowing will … a will that is full of destiny and purpose for us.)

The Lord knew that Joshua had a big task ahead of him, so He provided encouragement in Joshua 1:9: *"Be strong and of a good courage; be not afraid, neither be thou dismayed: for the LORD thy God is with thee whithersoever thou goest."* This Word from the Lord also holds a promise. The Lord said, "I am with you wherever you may go."

That promise is available to us as well. It's all going to be all right!

PRAYER OF COURAGE

Lord, today I declare that I am courageous. I declare that when adversity comes my way, I will not be faint of heart, but I will operate out of the courage You gave me. I will lean on and depend on You always. No trial or situation that comes my way will hinder me from walking in who You created me to be. I declare that I am victorious in every battle. I know You have equipped me to be strong and, as You told Joshua, to be of good courage. I will walk in courage and fear will not hinder me. In Jesus' Name I pray – Amen!

Confirmation

As we walk through this Christian journey, our relationship with God will be strengthened. The more we put into the relationship, the more we will reap from it. As the relationship grows, we will begin to hunger and thirst for God's will and power to operate in our lives. We will begin to listen for the voice of God, and move according to His voice. As we learn who God truly is, we will begin to know ourselves better because we are created in His image.

There will be times when God will show you things that will amaze you. I mentioned prayer in the last chapter. Prayer is the best tool to strengthen your relationship with God. Prayer is an open line of communication. It is conversation — not just you speaking, but God speaking as well. It's during these conversations that God will show you things about yourself and reveal the things He wants you to do … things you never thought you were capable of. You may think to yourself, "I can't do that." But, as you grow in the Lord and learn to trust Him, those things will come to pass.

Confirmation can come in several ways. Sometimes, God will tell you something, then share your assignment with a fellow Christian who will come along and tell you the same thing! See, the Holy Spirit will confirm what has already been established. Sometimes, it's the other way around: A Spirit-filled person will tell you something God wants you to do; then God will begin revealing to you the steps you need to take to accomplish it.

I would admonish you to be sure to seek God's approval for <u>all things</u>. There may be times when someone comes and speaks something into your life, but it doesn't settle well with your spirit. There will be people who confess to be of God, but whose motives are not aligned with the will of God. If someone tries to speak into your life, and you are not receiving it into your spirit, seek the Lord. He will be the one who brings final confirmation.

Each of us has access to the gifts of the Spirit, distributed by the Holy Spirit as He sees fit. Gifts of the Spirit are special abilities provided to Christians for the purpose of building up the body of Christ. 1 Corinthians 12:12-18 reveals that

> *For as the body is one, and hath many members, and all the members of that one body, being many, are one body: so also is Christ. For by one Spirit are we all baptized into one body, whether we be Jews or Gentiles, whether we be bond or free; and have been all made to drink into one Spirit. For the body is not one member, but many. If the foot shall say, Because I am not the hand, I am not of the body; is it therefore not of the body? And if the ear shall say, Because I am not the eye, I am not of the body; is it therefore not of the body? If the whole body were an eye, where were the hearing? If the whole were hearing, where were the smelling? But now hath God set the members every one of them in the body, as it hath pleased him.*

This passage of Scripture shows us that we are uniquely designed, but we all have a purpose in the Body of Christ. We each have our own unique set of gifts that brings pleasure and joy to our Creator.

In 1 Corinthians 12:8-10 we see the list of spiritual gifts, which includes wisdom, knowledge, faith, healing, miracles, prophecy, discerning of spirits, speaking in tongues, and interpretation of tongues. God does not want us to be ignorant of how He wants us to serve Him. He will equip us with whatever gifts of the Spirit we need to accomplish the tasks to which He has called us. Ephesians 4:11 chronicles the early-church assignments for what we know as the Fivefold Ministry: *"And he gave some, apostles; and some, prophets; and some, evangelists; and some, pastors and teachers."* There may be a different calling on our lives, but God will give us just what we need to fulfill what He wants us to do. If God calls you to be a teacher, for instance, He will gift you thusly.

But we must be open to serving God in other ways as well. We need to learn to serve God with all of who we are and go in whatever direction the Lord guides us. It is beneficial to know what spiritual gift(s) God has given us. We also need to be respectful of the gifts God has given our brothers and sisters in Christ. Romans 12:3 states that *"For I say, through the grace given unto me, to every man that is among you, not to think of himself more highly than he ought to think; but to think soberly, according as God hath dealt to every man the measure of faith."* We cannot become proud because of the gifts given us through the Holy Spirit, but we need to know how to celebrate one another's gifts. Focus on serving God with all obedience, and He will confirm within you and through others the steps you should take to fulfill His purpose for your life. Everything we do should be according to His will and for His glory and purpose. If we seek God's will and obey His leading, He will always equip us with whatever gifts we need.

PRAYER OF CONFIRMATION

Lord, I want to thank You for giving me an ear to hear Your voice. I thank You for revealing Yourself to me and showing me the life, You have set forth for me. I thank You for those who have come to confirm the assignments You have given me in our conversations, and I thank You for those obedient fellow servants who told me of assignments You had for me — assignments You later confirmed. I thank You for every gift You have given me. I want to serve You with all of me. In Jesus' Name I pray, Amen.

Character

Character is a big part of your Christian journey. Once you confess Christ and you are declared a Christian; people begin to watch your every move. Those who are not of the Kingdom will be watching to see if you mess up. But as we discussed in the previous lesson, we are freed from condemnation through Christ Jesus.

Character operates hand-in-hand with integrity. Both traits are built by doing things others don't like to do. As you walk in the counsel of the Almighty God, He will lead you to do such things. Do them, with integrity, for His honor and glory. You see, the greater the trial we face, the humbler we become as we get to the other side of that trial. Trials tend to prune us of our old, sinful ways and steer us God's way. In Malachi 3:2-3, the author speaks of the refiner's fire by saying: *"But who may abide the day of his coming? and who shall stand when he appeareth? for he is like a refiner's fire, and like fullers' soap: And he shall sit as a refiner and purifier of silver: and he shall purify the sons of Levi, and purge them as gold and silver, that they may offer unto the* LORD *an offering in righteousness."*
When gold and silver were put in the fire, all the impurities were burned away. The same is with us! As trials come and the fire is on us, we are being purified. Those old sins, those old mindsets, those old habits, and those old yokes are being burned

away from our lives. It is all part of the process. Sometimes that process involves great pain, but it is all for our good and God's glory. Have you ever noticed that before a slingshot launches, there is always a "pull back"? The one holding the slingshot pulls back even greater and harder so that the rocks launched by the slingshot will go farther and faster. If your purification process is uncomfortable or painful, don't lose heart. What looks like a drawback is actually positioning for a launching forward. Your character is being developed in the pull-back ... in the refiner's fire ... through the trials you face.

You'll find dramatic changes taking place once you yield everything to Christ. You will be faced with challenges that will pull you right out of your comfort zone. Say, for example, you grew up being an introvert, but then God calls you to walk in the shoes of an extrovert. You are now out of your comfort zone, so you face new challenges. Because you are outside of your comfort zone, the journey has become rocky. You are in unfamiliar territory, so things will be awkward at first. Let's say, for instance, that as an introvert you never said anything when you were hurt or mistreated. Now that you're in new territory, you make up your mind that this time it's going to be different and you will be more assertive. But you end up either coming on too strong and being perceived as obnoxious; or being a stammering, sputtering mess. You are silently screaming on the inside because you don't know what to do.

When you step outside your comfort zone to move in the things of God, people will judge you and even try to assassinate your character. You must strive to be fully yielded to God, developing your relationship with Him, or else you won't know how to handle the pressure. Acts 17:28 shows that *"For in him we live, and move, and have our being ..."* It's easy to get discouraged, to feel like giving up, to feel as though your passion is no longer there to keep you going ... to feel, in short, that you're losing the battle. You may feel invisible and unwanted. But deep inside, you know you must keep going. An internal battle is going on. You may feel caught between a rock and a hard place, not knowing what the next step will be. But you must learn to depend on God to guide you every step of the way. Don't go off on your own; allow Him to guide your footsteps. God will lead you, guide you and direct your steps (Proverbs 3:5-6). He will never leave you so that means He is always available for you.

People will look at you and try to condemn your actions based on what they see. But it doesn't matter what man sees, thinks, or says; it only matters what God says!

Let's briefly speak of the character of Peter. He left his career and followed Jesus. He had great faith and, as mentioned earlier, was the only other man besides Jesus who walked on water. But he had to go through some character-shaping. He had to be given an attitude adjustment when he rebuked Jesus for telling of His coming crucifixion. He had to be corrected when he at first refused to let Jesus wash his feet. Then he proved overprotective of Jesus in the Garden of Gethsemane; his temper flared up and he cut off the ear of Malchus, the servant of the high priest, when Jesus was arrested. Shortly afterward, Peter denied Jesus! But again, when Jesus returned to the earth from His victory in Hell and the order went out to notify the disciples of His resurrection, the only disciple mentioned specifically by name was Peter. One might think Peter had messed up too badly to be a disciple. He'd spoken before he thought, acted out of impulse, given into fear. But his character was being developed throughout all of this. He remained sold out for the sake of Christ. In Matthew 28, he and the other disciples were charged by Jesus to *"Go ye therefore, and teach all nations, baptizing them in the name of the Father, and of the Son, and of the Holy Ghost: Teaching them to observe all things whatsoever I have commanded you: and, lo, I am with you always, even unto the end of the world"* (Matt. 28:19-20).

Equipped with the Holy Spirit, Peter went on to fulfill this mission. We see in Acts 2, for instance, that he shared with the Jews:

- How the prophecies in the Old Testament had been fulfilled and victory gained.
- That God raised Jesus from the dead and the work of the cross was to save mankind from the sins it had committed.
- That if they repented of their sins and were baptized, they would receive the gift of the Holy Spirit.

Many would have written Peter off because of his actions during his character development. But God loves us and is always available to shape us into what He has designed us to be … in Peter's case, one of the most celebrated of the original 12 apostles.

Oftentimes it is when we are alone and able to get our thoughts together that revelation and understanding truly come. Being alone isn't a bad thing. Wanting always to be around others is a tactic of the enemy to keep us seeking love and acceptance from man. In actuality, God is the primary giver of love and acceptance, and He needs us alone with Him at times so that He can speak to us and show us what He wants us to do. Ask the Lord to put filters on your ears so that instead of being distracted by man, you heed the things God is telling and showing you. Then, allow your character to develop.

PRAYER FOR CHARACTER

Lord, I know that Your Word says we were created in Your image, and I just want to thank You for that. I thank You, Lord, that You don't give up on Your children and that You love us unconditionally. Lord, I ask You to help develop my character to be one that is pleasing and honorable to You.

Lord, I ask that I keep my eyes set on You; that the words from my mouth only bring You glory; that You protect the things I hear and let everything that my hands touch prosper for Your glory. In Jesus' Name I pray – Amen.

Compromise

Let's look at the Old Testament book of Daniel. What do Daniel and the three Hebrew boys — Hananiah, Mishael, and Azariah, also known as Shadrach, Meshach and Abednego — have in common? They refused to compromise!

We meet up with these young men after the nation of Judah was captured by Babylon. They were among the select young male captives chosen on order of King Nebuchadnezzar to be brought in and trained to serve in the palace.

Daniel, for whom the book is named, was an honest, hardworking man with great integrity. He was so set on his belief in the Lord, he chose not to compromise that belief. He went to serve under the Persian King Darius after Persia conquered Babylon. Many of the government officials became jealous of Daniel and tricked King Darius into putting a decree out across the land stating that anyone who prayed to another god or man besides the king for a 30-day period would be thrown into the lions' den. Daniel learned of the decree, but did not change his habit. Just as he had done all his life, he went home, knelt, faced Jerusalem, and prayed to God. He didn't hide and pray; he prayed boldly, with his windows open so that people could hear him. Some of those politicians and officials heard Daniel and told King Darius. The king loved Daniel and tried to save him, but the decree could not be revoked, so that night Daniel was placed in the den of lions. The king could not eat or sleep all night. When morning came, he ran to the den to check on Daniel. Daniel was still alive! He told the king that the Lord sent an angel to shut up the mouths of the lions. After this the king issued another decree, ordering the people to fear and reverence the God of Daniel.

See, Daniel could have given in and compromised his beliefs to please his captors. But he knew it was more profitable to follow the Lord. Daniel's refusal to compromise paid huge dividends!

Similar to Daniel's story is that of the three Hebrew boys: Shadrach, Meshach, and Abednego. In this story, Nebuchadnezzar built a huge golden image and commanded all the people to fall down and worship it whenever they heard the sound of his musical herald. Anyone who failed to bow and worship the image would be thrown into a blazing furnace. These three young men ignored the order and continued to worship the One true God; as a result, their actions were reported to the king. Boldly, they stood before the king as he pressed them to deny their God, but their response was recorded in Daniel 3:16-18: *"Shadrach, Meshach, and Abednego answered and said to the king, O Nebuchadnezzar, we are not careful to answer thee in this matter. If it be so, our God whom we serve is able to deliver us from the burning fiery furnace, and he will deliver us out of thine hand, O king. But if not, be it known unto thee, O king, that we will not serve thy gods, nor worship the golden image which thou hast set up."* It is here where we see not only the young men's faith, but their tenacity, determination and courage. They were not going to compromise their position in God.

Furious with pride and rage, Nebuchadnezzar ordered the furnace to be heated seven times hotter than normal. Shadrach, Meshach, and Abednego were bound and cast into the flames.

The fiery blast was so hot that it killed the soldiers who had escorted them into the furnace! But King Nebuchadnezzar had a surprise in store for him. In fact, he was nothing short of amazed when he looked into the furnace. Daniel 3:25 is his response: *"He answered and said, Lo, I see four men loose, walking in the midst of the fire, and they have no hurt; and the form of the fourth is like the Son of God."* When he called Shadrach, Meshach, and Abednego to come out of the furnace, they emerged looking like normal ... no singed hair, no burned clothes. They didn't even smell like smoke! The lesson here is that God will keep us protected when we stand for Him in the face of pressure from the world.

Chapter Three of Daniel ends with the awed king issuing another decree: Whomever spoke against the Hebrew men's God would be punished with death. Then he gave the men a job promotion!

Did you notice that both stories ended in the transformation of a nation due to those walking in the realness of God? They did not *compromise*. They walked with boldness and authority. They knew that God was and is in control and that no one, not even the king of the land where they were captive, could alter their belief. After Daniel was delivered from the lions, King Darius reversed his earlier decree and encouraged others to fear Daniel's Lord. In the story of the three young Hebrew men, we see a similar reaction from King Nebuchadnezzar. In Daniel 3:28, the king said, *"Blessed be the God of Shadrach, Meshach, and Abednego, who hath sent his angel, and delivered his servants that trusted in him, and have changed the king's word, and yielded their bodies, that they might not serve nor worship any god, except their own God."* Then in verse 29, he made his decree: Put your mouth on these men's God, and you die! Plus, your house will be turned into a dunghill!

Once you are converted to the ways of Christ, you are no longer the same inwardly. Your spirit has been instantly changed … you have become the "new man" (Ephesians 4:22-24). In the natural, however (your soul and body), you may still have some "old man" thinking and ways; those will change as your walk with Christ progresses. Sometimes your unsaved flesh will make you feel that by choosing Christ, you are missing out on the world's "fun." In reality, you are not missing anything. In Romans 12:1-2, Paul writes, *"I beseech you therefore, brethren, by the mercies of God, that ye present your bodies a living sacrifice, holy, acceptable unto God, which is your reasonable service. And be not conformed to this world: but be ye transformed by the renewing of your mind, that ye may prove what is that good, and acceptable, and perfect, will of God."* Once we receive Christ, we should be living for Him. This means there are things we may have done in the past that we should no longer be doing. There is a song by Troy Sneed titled, "Lay it Down." There are so many things that we need to lay down so that we can submit to Christ and live a life that is pleasing to Him.

The Bible makes it clear that God does not condone compromise: *"Joyful are people of integrity, who follow the instructions of the Lord. Joyful are those who obey His laws and search for Him with all their hearts. They do not compromise with evil, and they walk only in His paths"* (Psalm 119:1-3 NLT). We must give our all to Him because He has given His all to us. If we compromise, conforming to the ways of the world or the ways of the flesh, we may miss what God has for us. We want to be yielded and surrendered to Christ and carry on the work He established while on the earth. He, after all, is interceding on our behalf.

Ephesians 4:29-30 gives the admonition to *"let no corrupt communication proceed out of your mouth, but that which is good to the use of edifying, that it may minister grace unto the hearers. And grieve not the holy Spirit of God, whereby ye are sealed unto the day of redemption."* There are two main points I want to pull from this Scripture. The first is that you should not let corrupt communication come from your mouth — we should only be speaking those things that build up and edify. The second point is that you are not to grieve the Holy Spirit — if we compromise on our Christian witness, we will grieve the Holy Spirit by our actions. If we have learned the ways of the Lord and keep willfully sinning (compromising), the Bible says that *"it had been better for them not to have known the way of righteousness, than, after they have known it, to turn from the holy commandment delivered unto them"* (2 Peter 2:21).

Hebrews 10:22-26 also exhorts us as believers not to compromise our faith.

> ***Let us draw near with a true heart in full assurance of faith, having our hearts sprinkled from an evil conscience, and our bodies washed with pure water. Let us hold fast the profession of our faith without wavering; (for he is faithful that promised;) And let us consider one another to provoke unto love and to good works: Not forsaking the assembling of ourselves together, as the manner of some is; but exhorting one another: and so much the more, as ye see the day approaching. For if we sin wilfully after that we have received the knowledge of the truth, there remaineth no more sacrifice for sins.***

Here, the Lord is telling us to walk in love and draw near to Him. He is encouraging us to walk boldly in faith and not waver, and to provoke one another in love and do good works. If we have learned of these commands and opted to not obey them, there is no longer a reason for sacrifice.

PRAYER TO AVOID COMPROMISE

Lord, I thank You for Your Word and for those before me who were my examples ... examples of what we should do as believers, and examples of what we shouldn't do. I ask that You give me a determination and a tenacity to do all things according to Your ways. I do not want to waver; I want to be steadfast and immovable in my faith and devotion to You. I will not compromise the God in me for the pleasures of this world. I will not compromise my place in heaven to avoid any repercussions man may have for me should I not follow his direction. I declare that I am a child of the Lord Jesus Christ and I will allow Him to direct my steps. In Jesus' Name I pray – Amen!

Cultivation

To grow in this Christian journey, we need to learn how to die. That may sound like a strange statement, but it is the truth ... and the New Testament has several Scriptures that confirms it. You see, Jesus came to be our example and our guide to overcome the adversity we will encounter. Consider Paul's words in Galatians 2:20: *"I am crucified with Christ: nevertheless I live; yet not I, but Christ liveth in me: and the life which I now live in the flesh I live by the faith of the Son of God, who loved me, and gave himself for me."* We are being told that we cannot live according to the ways our flesh desires us to live if we are walking in the ways of Christ. If we continue to walk in our fleshly ways, we will be separated from Christ. But as we become dead to our own flesh and strive toward the ways of the Lord Jesus Christ, we enjoy life in Him.

In Luke 9:23-24, Jesus said, *"If any man will come after me, let him deny himself, and take up his cross daily, and follow me. For whosoever will save his life shall lose it: but whosoever will lose his life for my sake, the same shall save it."* By looking at this Scripture, we see that the ways of Christ are the polar opposite of the ways of the world. The world is consumed with the idea of getting as much as one can to be prosperous. But in this Scripture, we see that it's giving the Lord priority and denying ourselves and our desires that we gain great treasures in His Kingdom.

As we begin to learn who we are and what God desires of us, we will begin to die to who we thought we were and learn to trust God and His path for our lives. I think of the life of a seed that, when planted (buried), yields a harvest.

In John 3:16, we see that we gained eternal life when God gave His Son Jesus: *"For God so loved the world, that he gave his only begotten Son, that whosoever believeth in him should not perish, but have everlasting life."* Jesus was the seed God sent to the earth to save His creation ... you and me. Jesus came to die on the cross so that mankind could live. *"For the wages of sin is death; but the gift of God is eternal life through Jesus Christ our Lord" (Romans 6:23).*

Cultivation is a process in which farmers prepare the ground for planting crops by tilling (loosening) the soil. Loosening the ground creates an opportunity for growth to take place. After the seeds are planted, the farmer nurtures the ground by watering it and providing the proper nutrients needed for that crop to grow.

In John 12:24, we see that Jesus is telling the disciples that a seed must die to bring forth fruit. Let's look at this in more detail, as it may sound a little confusing.

A seed has a potential for life, but the Bible tells us it must die to bring forth life. What? Let me explain it so you will really understand what the Word of God is teaching us. The seed is planted, and now it begins to undergo a process. The watering of the soil, and the provision of nutrients, now brings forth a sprout. This sprout is a sign that life has evolved. But let's keep our focus on that seed that was planted. If we dig up the sprout, will we find the seed? Nope. The seed has died; it ceased being a seed so that the sprout could live. The seed sacrificed its life so that new life could come. The word "sacrifice" is defined as an act of giving up something of value for the sake of something else regarded as more important and worthy. In the sprout, we see that the potential for life that lay in the seed has brought forth new life. For new life to come forth, cultivation had to take place, making the right environment for this seed to die and then produce life. The seed couldn't do it on its own ... the environment had to be prepared and then the seed planted, nurtured and nourished. This process doesn't take place immediately.

The seed endures a period of dormancy. After this period, the sprout comes forth through a process called germination.

In the Kingdom of God, we, too, are seeds. We must die to ourselves to follow the ways of the Lord. Our desire to be in a fruitful relationship with Him will make us want, and allow, our lives to be cultivated to the ways of the Lord. A few other definitions of the word "cultivate" means to give special attention to; to improve or foster, as to study or educate and to acquire; or to develop as in quality, sentiment, or skills. We have to allow the ways of the Lord to germinate — grow and flourish — in our lives.

As we begin to grow from within, there will be things in our lives that will also die. Things that are not of God, things that have been hidden deep within our beings will need to be cultivated — dug up and loosened so that they will be exposed to the light of Christ. Trust the Lord and know that these things are being exposed only to cause you to die to self and learn to depend on the Lord Jesus Christ, your Savior. Once this process takes place, healing will manifest. We'll find that desires of the past will no longer fit in our new life, and we will no longer want to continue our bad habits. Our minds will have made a transformation ... our old ways will give way to our new ways.

We will begin to walk in the new freedom we have been given by the Lord.

There will need to be a pruning to rid us of the dead things that are trying to stay attached to us … things that are no longer relevant to our lives. Sometimes this pruning stage can be difficult, but it is necessary. We cannot successfully walk in the will of our Lord and Saviour with this dead debris attached to us. We must allow it to be cut away so that we can be effective in what the Lord wants to do in us and through us for His Kingdom.

As you nurture and cultivate your relationship with the Lord, ask Him to identify things within you that need to be removed. He has given us our own will, but it's His desire that you lay down your life for Him, and that your will be in alignment with His. It's a conscious choice we have to make daily. When we are seeking Him for all things, we are fostering a relationship with Him and as we do so, we are bringing Him pleasure. Our actions are telling Him that we want what He wants for us in life.

As your relationship with the Lord grows, protect it with prayer. Prayer is a weapon in spiritual warfare and believe me when I say that once you begin your upward movement in the ways of the Lord, you will be on the radar of the enemy and he will seek to devour you. Prayer is the key to winning the battle. It does not matter how bad a situation may seem … remember that the Lord has promised several times in His Word that He will never leave us nor forsake us. This means that He is always around to call on.

Know that Satan will try to plant his own seeds in your cultivated soil. He will mix his seeds of deceit and deception in with your good seeds to make you lose focus of what the Lord has spoken to you and keep you from moving toward your purpose and destiny. It's important to learn the ways of the Lord so that we can walk in our identity of Him, having been created in His image. But it's also important to be wise to the ways of Satan — an adversary of the Lord who will do anything to cause the children of the Lord to go off-track and wander outside of the will of the Lord.

This isn't anything I am making up; it's something the Lord showed through a parable in Matthew 13:24-30. He told of a farmer who had sown good seeds. During the night, however, his enemy came and sowed some seeds along with the farmer's good seeds. As the crops began to grow, the field hands realized that there were two different types of harvest coming forth. They told the farmer. He told them to let the wheat and the tares grow together; the bad seed (tares) would be done away with at harvest. Learn how to recognize the bad seeds – from simple fear and doubt to the reappearance of those who represent the past toxic relationships of your old life — and deal with them at the appointed time. Don't allow them to overtake you ... know that you have the power and authority to overtake them. Everything you need is within you, planted by the spirit of the Lord Jesus Christ when you confessed Him as Lord and Savior over your life. Cultivate that relationship and allow it to flourish.

PRAYER OF CULTIVATION

Lord, Your Word is alive. It is clear that I need to die to self, but You desire this so that I may live the life You have predestined for me. Lord, give me a heart to cultivate a relationship with You. Transform me that I may be a living sacrifice to You, just as a seed is a living sacrifice for its purpose of producing life. Use me for a purpose that is pleasing and acceptable to You and You alone. In Jesus' Name I pray, Amen.

Correction

I was going to incorporate correction with cultivation. As I began to expound upon cultivation, the Lord showed me that correction needed its own section.

Let's begin in 1 Corinthians 14:40, which says, *"Let all things be done decently and in order."* The Kingdom of God has established order and guidelines to follow. These are known as commandments. One definition of a commandment: an important rule given by God that tells people how to behave. In the Old Testament, God gives us the 10 Commandments. Then, in the New Testament, we learn that love is the greatest commandment.

Although we are children of God, we are apt to make errors from time to time. It's a part of life. Romans 3:23 tells us, *"For all have sinned, and come short of the glory of God"*; therefore, correction is needed. Correction is used to get us back on track and give us an opportunity to learn from our mistakes.

Correction is given for various reasons. Protection is one of the main ones. Those of us with children in their lives have all experienced times when we have had to bring correction for this purpose. For example, I once had a 4-year-old boy with me during a trip to the store. When we exited the car, he took off running from the car to the store. I had to call him back to me and explain that he was to look both ways before venturing into an area where cars regularly pass. I did this to protect him.

Protection is what God provides for us, His children. He wants us to have the best things in life. As your relationship with God is cultivated, you will begin to hear Him more and more. He will lead, guide, and correct you through the Holy Spirit Who lives on the inside of you. God's correction is referenced in such Scriptures as Proverbs 3:11 (*My son, despise not the chastening of the Lord; neither be weary of his correction.*)

During your Christian walk, God will sometimes use those in spiritual authority over you, such as your pastor, to correct you. Pastors have a calling to watch over the flock and give correction to help bring improvement in the lives of members.

There are four components needed to properly bring correction. First, correction must be done wisely. In 2 Timothy 2:20-26 we see God's instruction for how to deal with correction in a wise manner.

> ***But in a great house there are not only vessels of gold and of silver, but also of wood and of earth; and some to honour, and some to dishonour. If a man therefore purge himself from these, he shall be a vessel unto honour, sanctified, and meet for the master's use, and prepared unto every good work. Flee also youthful lusts: but follow righteousness, faith, charity, peace, with them that call on the Lord out of a pure heart. But foolish and unlearned questions avoid, knowing that they do gender strifes. And the servant of the Lord must not strive; but be gentle unto all men, apt to teach, patient, In meekness instructing those that oppose themselves; if God peradventure will give them repentance to the acknowledging of***

the truth; And that they may recover themselves out of the snare of the devil, who are taken captive by him at his will.

In this Scripture, God is instructing the pastor and other leaders on how to deal with dishonorable behavior. There are some things that will need to be addressed for the truth to be revealed and for the individual to be released from the snares of the enemy.

Once the truth is revealed to us in wisdom, we have a mandate to walk in that truth, which is for our benefit. In John 8:32 the Bible says, *"And ye shall know the truth, and the truth shall make you free."* If you have a teachable spirit and receive your pastor's instruction and correction, you will be able to freely walk in the ways of the Lord. In James 4:17, the Word reveals that *"Therefore to him that knoweth to do good, and doeth it not, to him it is sin."* What this Scripture shows us is that once you have been exposed to the truth and you fail to abide by that truth, you are choosing to walk in sin. Ideally, as your relationship with the Lord grows, your heart will be drawn to what is right. Those things that used to get you off track won't bother you anymore. You will have to be able to walk in self-control. That is why it's so important that those God uses to correct you must impart that correction wisely … with patience, gentleness, and meekness as indicated in 2 Timothy, but in firmness.

The second component for properly giving correction is that it must be done in love. It's not always easy for pastors or leaders to bring correction. It may hurt them to have to do it as much as it may hurt you to receive it, but it must be done. A leader that is operating in the spirit of the Lord will bring correction in a loving way.

I have received unloving treatment from a pastor under the guise of correction. I was in a place of transition, moving from one state to another so that I could reestablish myself; meanwhile, I was renting the pastor's basement temporarily. This pastor — who did not want me to leave and upset because I wouldn't change my mind — got in front of the congregation and spoke of having made a mistake regarding me. "I don't know where she is going to sleep tonight because she can't come back to my house," the pastor declared. As the pastor spoke, I felt like a knife was twisting in my chest. I was told, also in front of the congregation, that if I moved away, I would be giving up and would be seen as a failure. I realized that the "correction" wasn't coming from a position of love, but from a position of retaliation and control. We must remember that even if they are called by God to do His work, pastors are still human and have flesh to deal with. They need to check the spirit from which their urge to correct is coming.

I have also received genuine, beneficial correction from another pastor who showed sincerity and love. There was no malice in the correction, just a desire to help create positive changes in me for the benefit of the Kingdom. After the correction comes and it has been done in love, you will be thanking that person. You will walk away thanking the Lord for the knowledge and insight it takes to be effective in Him.

Correction should not be quarrelsome; it must be kind and done in gentleness. The one bringing the correction has to prepare well; their motives are often challenged if the person being corrected is not willing to accept correction. Correction won't be effective if it is antagonistic, i.e., with a motive is to set someone straight or prove them wrong. That's what was happening in my bad experience with the first pastor. The pastor was upset and seeking to humiliate me.

Thirdly, correction must be based on the Word of God. When correction is coming forth, the one who is bringing it should show you the Scriptures that defend the purpose of the correction. The Scriptures will point out the act that has prompted the correction, and they will show the proper method of correction. Scriptures showing how God forgives can be used, but the key is that the process will be based on the Word of God and not how the one bringing correction feels things should go.

Finally, correction must be made and received with awareness of spiritual warfare. We need to understand that there are two forces in this world … the Lord and His adversary, the devil. An adversary is one's opponent in a contest, conflict, or dispute. The devil is always in competition with God. His plan is to steal, kill, and destroy any plan that the Lord has established. This is why correction is necessary. The devil's modus operandi is to tempt God's people into incorrect patterns of thought and behavior and detour them from God's plan for their lives. We have to realize that we are struggling against the spiritual forces of wickedness in the heavenly places (Ephesians 6:12) and heed anyone who offers loving correction to help us back on track when the devil tries to derail us.

In all situations, seek God! If someone brings correction, ask the Lord if that person's spirit is right. He will let you know whether that correction is in your best interest.

PRAYER FOR CORRECTION

Lord, I thank You for the commands and instructions You have provided me in Your Word. I want to develop a time of consecration and dedication to learn Your Word so that I may order my life in obedience to You. I do understand that due to my human nature, there will be times where I will fall short of Your commands. I want to thank You in advance for assigning true vessels in Your Kingdom to lead me back to You through loving correction and wise counsel. You are the Lord of my life and it is my desire to please You in all I do, so I openly welcome correction and insight as to how I can become all You created me to be. In Jesus' Name I pray, Amen.

Commitment

One day on my way to work, I was in deep thought. I was thinking of the Old Testament account in which King David impregnated Bathsheba and tried to cover it up.

In this account, found in 2 Samuel 11, David sent for Bathsheba's husband Uriah, who was away at war. He reasoned that Uriah would come home and have relations with his wife; then when her pregnancy became evident, he would think it was his child. When Uriah came, he gave a report to David about the events of the war. Then David instructed Uriah to go home and wash his feet. When David woke up in the morning, he realized that Uriah had not gone home; rather he'd stayed at the door of the king's house. David asked Uriah why he didn't go home. An upright and noble man, Uriah explained that the Ark of the Covenant, along with the men of Israel and Judah, and Joab the commander, were abiding in tents and open fields and that it would not be fair that he was able to go home. David got Uriah drunk, but Uriah still did not go home. Finally, David sent Uriah back to the battlegrounds with a note to Joab, instructing that Uriah be sent to the front lines and to keep him there until he dies. And that's what happened.

There were parts of the story I knew, but I had to go and reread to see all the elements that occurred. I came away with a word: "Don't let your commitment kill you." In other words, you need to ask the Lord for discernment to know which things you should commit to, and which things you should not. Proverbs 3:5-6 tells us, *"Trust in the LORD with all thine heart; and lean not unto thine own understanding. In all thy ways acknowledge him, and he shall direct thy paths."* We should not make any moves or decisions without first consulting the Lord, to Whom we should primarily be committed so that His purpose for our lives will come to pass. He will place us within a ministry to which He would have us commit. Uriah wasn't placed in a ministry, but he joined with a group and became committed to the task at hand. It was through David's deception that Uriah ended up losing his life. Although we may not lose our lives like he did, variations of this scenario can happen to us all too easily. That is why it is so important to seek the Lord before we commit to anything.

We have already spoken about compromise. Uriah didn't compromise; he was an honorable man who did not deserve the fate he suffered. At the end of this story, in the last sentence of 2 Samuel 11, we see that, "t*he thing that David had done displeased the LORD."* Uriah was honorable, but David was dishonorable ... and God held David accountable. We never want to displease God and grieve the Holy Spirit, so we want to be sure to seek God's direction, God's guidance, God's ways, and God's will. Our lives should be all about Him.

Once God shows you where to commit yourself, there sometimes must be a sacrifice. This may mean you will have to make an investment of your time, talent, or treasure (money) at a higher level that you'd planned or desired. You will have to come to the realization that you aren't working for earthly vessels who are giving you direction. Rather, you are working for God and with God. The tasks you are given may seem menial, but there is no such thing as a menial task in the Kingdom of God. Do your work with diligence and dedication. You must be responsible and accountable for the tasks assigned.

I remember an instance in which a person I knew was given an assignment, but lacked all the information needed to complete the task. Instead of asking me for the information, this person came to me and asked me to complete the assignment for them. This is where accountability and responsibility come in. What if I had decided I didn't want to perform the task, and the assignment had gone uncompleted? I wouldn't have gotten in trouble because it wasn't my assignment in the first place.

Sometimes God gives you tasks to see if you will take responsibility for them. If you exhibit a cycle of sloughing your responsibilities onto others, you are ineffective in your assignment at best and a hindrance at worst. Being committed to something means you are in it for the duration and that you are determined to complete the task.

Sometimes we commit to the wrong things. Again, you will need the Lord's help to discern the spirits of those with whom you are partnering. When you become committed to a cause, some people will try to compete with you, some will try to pull from you and drain you, some will want you to jump ship and come work with them, and some will become intimidated by you and try to hinder you from continuing. You need to learn how to recognize when these things are happening, and learn how to seek God as to how He wants you to proceed. Don't get upset and abandon your assignment; seek the Father and He will lead you.

When I lived in Minnesota, I had a friend who told her pastor about my administrative abilities. Eventually, her pastor contacted me and told me that she wanted me to help her get her school of ministry started. She told me that my friend had referred me and was telling her of my abilities. As I communicated with her, I felt in my spirit that the pastor was trying to draw me away from what I was currently doing. So, I boldly told her, "I can possibly assist you, but I cannot allow it to interfere with what I am currently doing at my own church."

The pastor didn't like my answer. But as she was sharing what she wanted me to do, the Lord was showing me the truth behind it. I knew I could not compromise in any area, nor could I lose focus of the commitments God had already given me. I could not move without the permission of the Lord.

Here's another story to show the importance of knowing where, and to whom God would have you commit. I was part of an organization for which I had a weekly task that, during one particular year, claimed my Saturdays from April through the first weekend of August. I completely loved what I was doing; it didn't even bother me to give up my Saturdays because I saw the value of my work and the effect it had on the lives of the people involved. One week, however, I had to be out of town. I took my trip, returned home and fell right back into my assignment, not missing a beat. But one of the program participants called several individuals in my life and began to spread lies about me and my devotion to my task. I got upset and was ready to throw in the towel. But the Lord would not let me abandon my assignment. I had about four more weeks before it would be completed, and only after those four weeks would He release me. I couldn't let my hurt feelings stop me from carrying out my responsibilities, so I just "sucked it up" and carried on. When the summer program was over, however, I packed up everything related to it and returned it to the organization and explained to its leaders that it was my time to leave the organization.

As in my case, there are going to be times when you get upset or even frustrated about a situation. But that does not give you permission to abandon your assignment or lessen your commitment. We cannot submit to our flesh; we need to abide by the spirit of the Lord to stay committed to Him.

When it comes to commitment, there must be a balance. I am one who will run myself crazy in order to complete a task. If I commit myself to a task, I will do all that is within me to accomplish that task. I try my hardest to be a person of my word; if I said I will do it; I will do all I can to get it done. I enjoy bringing people pleasure and joy and hate to let them down. But, as I said, there must be balance. Again, it's about seeking direction from the Lord.

Commitment is not always easy. Those who are married will attest to this; marriage is a major commitment. This is true, however, in any relationship, whether it be husband/wife, mother/daughter, brother/sister, sister/sister, pastor/member, supervisor/employee, and so forth ... Any time two people are tasked with something together, the potential for discord is possible. That doesn't always have to be the case, but we each have our own minds and our own ways of thinking. The good news is that through God all things are made possible. We can be victorious through the power of communication and commitment.

Before we close, let's look at Jesus and the sense of commitment He possessed. He was already in heaven with His Father, but He agreed to leave, come down to earth and fulfill the law by becoming a sacrifice to save mankind. He knew before He even left heaven that He was required to die. While He was here on earth, He faced many trials and tribulations ... just as we face them today. Jesus was our example on how to face trials and tribulations the way in which the Father desired us to do. The people lied about Jesus, arrested, beat and tortured Him and, eventually, crucified Him. Some of those who'd followed Jesus earlier turned their backs on Him. But Jesus was committed to the purpose for which He'd been called to this earth realm. He was even tempted by Satan himself, but Jesus did not bow down to Satan or man. He stood firmly on the foundation of the Word of God. When Jesus was hanging on the cross, He could have called the Father to come rescue Him, but He know the weight of the purpose of the cross. So instead, He began to ask the Father to "forgive them, for they know not what they do" (Luke 23:34). This story is so powerful. Jesus didn't have to do it, but He chose to be crucified just for you. He was committed.

Follow Jesus' lead and commit yourself to God, not to man. But, first and foremost, make sure you have committed yourself in a ministry to which He has sent you. Whereas Jesus sacrificed His life in the right assignment, don't lose your life in the wrong one!

PRAYER OF COMMITTMENT

Lord, I commit myself to You and Your ways. I commit myself to the purpose and destiny You laid before me as You were creating me in my mother's womb, and I commit myself to the work of the ministry. I take each assignment with great honor and yield to You. I will continue to seek You for direction, as well as discernment, when making decisions. I do not want to be out of order in any way; rather, I want to be submitted to You in all my ways. When I receive an assignment from You, I will take responsibility for completing it with all You have placed within me. In Jesus' Name I pray, Amen.

Clutter/Chatter

As you begin to walk in what God has for you, beware of spiritual clutter.

Clutter is the lies the enemy feeds to you to distract you. Clutter is the enemy taking the negative things in your past and making them seem current. Specifically, clutter is the enemy hindering you in your now by reminding you of how people hurt you in the past … especially in settings and situations that resemble those in which you were hurt. The enemy's goal is to isolate you so that he can prey on your mind and keep you from being effective.

In short, clutter is a tactic the enemy uses to get you to abort God's plans for you.

As you grow in Christ, you will experience instances of misunderstanding and unsurety. The key to navigating your way through them is to seek the Heavenly Father for insight and understanding. Apply His word to each situation.

Let's look at Ephesians 6:10-20. Verse 10 says, *"Finally, my brethren, be strong in the Lord, and in the power of his might."* This verse shows that the Lord already knows you will be in adversity. Paul, the author of Ephesians, points out that you are to be strong in the power that the Lord displays and makes available to you and for you on your behalf. You cannot be strong on your own; you can only be strong through the strength of the Lord. Paul then goes on to instruct us in what we need to do in order to be effectively guarded. Let's look at verses 11-18.

> *Put on the whole armour of God, that ye may be able to stand against the wiles of the devil. For we wrestle not against flesh and blood, but against principalities, against powers, against the rulers of the darkness of this world, against spiritual wickedness in high places. Wherefore take unto you the whole armour of God, that ye may be able to withstand in the evil day, and having done all, to stand. Stand therefore, having your loins girt about with truth, and having on the breastplate of righteousness; And your feet shod with the preparation of the gospel of peace; Above all, taking the shield of faith, wherewith ye shall be able to quench all the fiery darts of the wicked. And take the helmet of salvation, and the sword of the Spirit, which is the word of God: Praying always with all prayer and supplication in the Spirit, and watching thereunto with all perseverance and supplication for all saints.*

The armor of God is the protection of God. The armor of God is a metaphor for the actions we need to take in our spiritual lives to protect us against the wiles of the enemy ... the principalities, the powers, and the rulers of the dark world that have waged war against God. As followers of God, we become targets. The Lord knew we would face many battles. Oftentimes the battles we face are not just about us personally, but about the enemy's goal to keep the will of God from being manifested in this earth realm.

We have all seen a pyramid hierarchy. This describes the Kingdom of God. God the Father is seated at the top of this pyramid. Then there is Jesus, the One who intercedes for us. The next layer is a compounded layer that consists of the fivefold ministry gifts and those who operate in them. This layer is compounded because the gift holders carry the indwelling of the Holy Spirit, also part of the triune being of God. The next layer consists of the workers of the Kingdom, who help support the ministry gifts and fulfill the vision the Lord has given them to accomplish.

What the devil likes to do is go to us, the workers, and distract us, filling our minds with clutter. If we don't submit fully to the Lord and allow Him to have dominion over the situation, the clutter will derail us so that we will be ineffective in the Body of Christ. This can have a domino effect, detouring the fulfillment of God's plan through the ministry gifts. (That is why, in verse 18, we are told to pray always with supplication in the spirit. Supplication means to ask or beg for something earnestly or humbly.)

Clutter causes us to get upset and begin to talk ...or, as I call it, chatter. The chatter may take the form of gossip, which causes even more clutter in our minds. It's a vicious cycle in which the enemy wants us to be trapped.

But in Ephesians 6:10, we are told to be strong in the power of the Lord. You see, many of us *know* the word, but fail to *activate* the word. When a new credit card comes in the mail, it must be activated in order for us to use it. If it is not activated at the time we need it, it's unusable. It's the same thing with the Word of God. We have to activate His Word so that it can be fruitful in our lives.

Let's look at Proverbs 6:16-19:

> ***These six things doth the LORD hate: yea, seven are an abomination unto him: A proud look, a lying tongue, and hands that shed innocent blood, An heart that deviseth wicked imaginations, feet that be swift in running to mischief, A false witness that speaketh lies, and he that soweth discord among brethren.***

If these are the things God hates, then these are the things we should avoid as we go through our Christian journey. The very things the Lord hates – pride, lying, hurting the innocent, scheming, making mischief, destroying another's good name, causing conflict or disharmony among others — are the very things the devil will try to tempt you to do. That, again, is why we must always be praying. In 1 Thessalonians 5:17, we are told to *"pray without ceasing."* We can't get weary; we must remain strong – which we can do in the power of the Lord's might. We must be humble enough to know where our strength ends and where His strength takes over. Actually, what strength we have isn't even our own, but that which has been given us through the Father. So again, we need to depend on Him.

If we submit to the Father, He will remove the clutter. He will remove the heavy burdens that weigh us down. He will remove the yokes that keep us in bondage. If we can do all things through Christ who strengthens us, we need to believe that the Lord can do the impossible in our lives.

Don't lose yourself in clutter. Resist the temptation to chatter; if you need to speak, speak to the Lord.

I remember going through an issue that involved someone else. I felt that I needed to speak to this person directly about the problem; if I spoke to anyone else, I would feel as though I was gossiping. (In Matthew 18: 15-17, we are told that if we have an ought against someone, we should go to that person.) My request to discuss things with this person was, unfortunately, ignored multiple times. Because of this, I allowed bitterness and resentment to enter my heart; these came accompanied by chatter ... and only made the issue worse. After several years of torment from the enemy, I learned that the Lord is the one who will listen when no one else will! His Word tells us in many places that He will never leave us nor forsake us. You see, men may forsake you because they think they have you figured out. But the Lord knows us better then we know ourselves; after all, He is our Creator. So, take your broken pieces to the Manufacturer. He will show you exactly what is needed. Don't be too proud to go before the Lord!

Just know that there will be times when you may go through something and feel you just need that one person that you go to that will offer you advice, encouragement or just a listening ear. We have to be careful in these times as well. While it is good to have your brothers and/or sisters encourage you, you can't just give information that will harm the character of someone else. You need to evaluate your motive before talking to anyone and if you aren't sure what you should say and shouldn't say, turn your conversation to God. If you're speaking to Him, it won't be chatter (gossip) because He already knows all.

The Bible tells us in Galatians 6:7, *"Be not deceived; God is not mocked: for whatsoever a man soweth, that shall he also reap."* Oftentimes we sow bad seeds and when the harvest of trials and tribulations come, we are a mess; this is where clutter begins to hinder us to keep us down. So many times, we want to blame the devil when he didn't do anything — we sowed the seeds and the harvest came. (The devil, of course, does not mind being in the limelight and receiving the credit.)

There's plenty that Satan *will* do to derail you and discredit your walk with Christ. He will use every tool possible to bring you down. Don't let something so simple as clutter be the thing that will allow the devil a foothold in your life. God has so much more in store for us than we can ever imagine, so don't fall to the temptation of the enemy.

I realize that this is sometimes easier said than done. I have fallen into this trap and even initiated it. You see, you can participate in two ways: you start it or you receive it. Either way, you are guilty. If this is the case with you, seek the Lord's forgiveness, then change (repent) and continue in your walk with Him. Another step you may need to take, depending on the situation, is going to the person you chattered about and apologizing. When you apologize, you must do so with sincerity. Then, you must activate your faith for permanent change (repentance).

At all times, be mindful of your weaknesses and seek the Lord to strengthen you. Protect yourself; other than the Lord, no one will protect you better than you. You can't cast out a spirit in which you actively operate. Repentance and a change of ways will enable you to cast it out properly. You cannot be a double agent, working for the Kingdom of God while operating in the kingdom of darkness. The Bible speaks to this in Matthew 6:24: *"No man can serve two masters: for either he will hate the one, and love the other; or else he will hold to the one, and despise the other. Ye cannot serve God and mammon."*

In closing, I would emphasize that we need to do as the Bible instructs us to do in Philippians 4:8: *"Finally, brethren, whatsoever things are true, whatsoever things are honest, whatsoever things are just, whatsoever things are pure, whatsoever things are lovely, whatsoever things are of good report; if there be any virtue, and if there be any praise, think on these things."* We must change our thinking. We have to recognize the source of every thought and rebuke those that we know are not of God (remember 1 Corinthians 10:5 – *"Casting down imaginations, and every high thing that exalteth itself against the knowledge of God, and bringing into captivity every thought to the obedience of Christ"*). The way to overcome a cluttered mind is to try your thoughts by the Word of God. If they align, follow the command. If they don't align, cast them into the pit of hell and seek the Lord on how to handle the situation at hand.

I often am driving when seeking the Lord. One day I was seeking Him about this chapter on clutter and chatter. The song "Great Exchange" by Martha Munizzi came on the car stereo and began to speak to me. Let's look at the chorus:

> ***This is the great exchange***
> ***I'm trading my sorrow***
> ***for the coming of grace***
> ***Heaven is opened***
> ***every time I praise***
> ***This is the great,***
> ***This is the great exchange***

The enemy wants to keep us bound up with a cluttered mind. Having a cluttered mind keeps you from praying; therefore, "the great exchange" cannot occur. Instead, you feel that there is a wall that's blocking you from seeking the Lord. You are pressing, but you feel you are not getting anywhere. But it's in the pressing that release comes. The pressing of the olive is when the oil is released. We too must be pressed so that the anointing God has placed within us comes out. In 2 Corinthians 4:8-10 we find that *"We are troubled on every side, yet not distressed; we are perplexed, but not in despair; Persecuted, but not forsaken; cast down, but not destroyed; Always bearing about in the body the dying of the Lord Jesus, that the life also of Jesus might be made manifest in our body."*

We gather clutter in our minds by failing to renew them. We cannot be like hoarders and fail to clean out our homes (minds). We cannot live in the flesh and allow clutter to rule; we have the power to cast it out. In Romans 7, we see that Paul, a strong man in the Lord, still had battles with the flesh. We all will face those battles. Just know that the Lord is on your side because you are His. Keep your faith and protect yourself through God and through His love.

PRAYER TO REMOVE CLUTTER AND CHATTER

Lord, I come to You now knowing that I have not operated according to Your Word, and I ask You to forgive me for the wrongs I have done. I repent of any wickedness I have allowed to enter my life. I ask that You purify my heart, my mind and my tongue; cleanse me of all unrighteousness; and renew Your spirit within me. Please direct my steps and guide me in Your ways. I ask for blessings for anyone against whom I have spoken. In Jesus' Name I pray, Amen.

Captivity

The word "captivity" is defined at Dictionary.com as "being held, imprisoned, enslaved, or confined." You can't freely move about when you are in captivity. You will not be able to grow properly if you are being held captive.

In 2015, I turned 40 years old. It was my sincere prayer at that time that I would not carry anything that kept me bound in my younger years into this new decade of life ... and there were many things that had kept me bound.

I began to hear the Lord telling me to share my testimony, but I immediately became scared. I would share portions of it via various Facebook posts, but never the whole story. I began to dream of sharing my testimony. There were many nights during which I had those dreams ... dreams so vivid, it seemed like I was awake. As I shared in those dreams, it was like I'd cut open my heart and poured everything out. In these dreams, my sharing didn't come from a place of hurt, but a place of power and authority. I was bragging on how God brought me out! But then, I would wake up and still feel bound by my fear.

I remember one night in which we had a deliverance service at church. I heard the Lord say, "This is the night to share." Instead of being obedient and stepping out, I just stayed in my place and began to cry. The devil began to tell me, "These people don't want to hear about what you have been through." Fear had me in such a tight grip that I could not move.

About a week later, I was in church again. It was near the end of service; there were a few people there. We'd had prayer. I asked if I could share something and, given permission, I began to share. It was nothing like I had dreamed, but I finally was able to share some things. There is a difference between sharing something while chatting on a computer and standing before people and confessing it with your mouth. As I was sharing, however, the spirit in the room changed. It felt as though what I was saying didn't even matter to the listeners; they just wanted to go home. So, I cut the testimony short. I turned the microphone back over to the meeting facilitator, who then remarked, "I've heard that before." These words felt like a knife to my heart.

After this occurred, I went to the Lord. "I did what you said; why didn't it work?" I asked. "Why is it that I feel worse now than I did before?"

God revealed to me that the audience wasn't the right audience. Everything we do has to be according to God's timing, not our own. Healing will come in God's time, not ours.

The dreams still came. In them I would still share my story with power and authority. But in real life, I was in a foggy stage.

I began to do a study on the steps I needed to take to be delivered. During this study, I began to write out as confessions those things I had done in my past. I began to denounce, in Jesus' name, those spirits that kept me bound. I told Satan and his imps that they had no control over my life. I worked about a week, writing out the confessions of every sin I believe I had ever committed, even if they were just thoughts. I recorded these sins because I so badly wanted to be free that I didn't want to leave as much as a toehold for the enemy to creep back in.

I knew that deliverance was a powerful topic and if not done correctly, I could end up in even worse condition. As I began to communicate with the Lord about when and how to go about self-deliverance, I began to realize I did not want to do this at home. I had to protect my family from any demonic spirits that might try to transfer from me to my family members. Demons are strong forces, and I wanted to protect those I love.

Let's look at Matthew 8:28-32 and learn how these spirits operate when they are cast out.

> *And when he was come to the other side into the country of the Gergesenes, there met him two possessed with devils, coming out of the tombs, exceeding fierce, so that no man might pass by that way. And, behold, they cried out, saying, What have we to do with thee, Jesus, thou Son of God? art thou come hither to torment us before the time? And there was a good way off from them an herd of many swine feeding. So the devils besought him, saying, If thou cast us out, suffer us to go away into the herd of swine. And he said unto them, Go. And when they were come out, they went into the herd of swine: and, behold, the whole herd of swine ran violently down a steep place into the sea, and perished in the waters.*

In this Scripture, we see that Jesus cast the demons out of the men; the demons then fled to the pigs, which ended up drowning in the water. I was taking was a stance to cast out demons, so I had to ensure that they did not flee into a family member or even my pets. I knew that, due to the power and authority we have given through Christ Jesus, we can dictate where demons could flee.

In Luke 10:19 the Word of God tells us, *"Behold, I give unto you power to tread on serpents and scorpions, and over all the power of the enemy: and nothing shall by any means hurt you."* I knew that the prayer I had prepared would cause the demons to flee, and I wanted to ensure that I did everything according to how the Lord wanted it to be done. So, after work this particular Friday, I went to the church alone. This is nothing that I hadn't done before — I used to go to the church alone to pray all the time after work or between appointments. But this time, things felt so different. There was such urgency from within me to get there and do what I needed to do. The deliverance prayer had three different sections. The first section was the one in which all the confessions were made. The second section involved calling upon the Lord for strength and covering. The final section involved speaking directly to Satan proclaiming those things he had stolen from me that he could no longer keep.

As I began to pray, I was met with many distractions, even though I was alone. Praying the prayer felt awkward. The room felt extremely hot. I could not get my words out properly. I heard a noise in another part of the church. Even after I prayed the first two sections, I had to prepare myself for the third section.

Finally, I prayed that final part of the prayer. And, despite the awkwardness, I felt different! It worked — thank you Lord, I was free! Right? Wrong.

Let's look at Luke 11:24-26: *"When the unclean spirit is gone out of a man, he walketh through dry places, seeking rest; and finding none, he saith, I will return unto my house whence I came out. And when he cometh, he findeth it swept and garnished. Then goeth he, and taketh to him seven other spirits more wicked than himself; and they enter in, and dwell there: and the last state of that man is worse than the first."* As we discussed in the chapter about cycles, that big ball of tape was happening.

After the initial prayer of deliverance, I continued to pray, but probably not as fervently as I should have. The demons returned, bigger in number and stronger than before. I truly felt like I was drowning. I reached out for help several times, but was told I couldn't be babysat. People would watch me and begin to speak things upon me. You can't be quick to receive what everyone tells you; you have to study it for yourself, so I would do a study on the things being said in order to learn whether they were the truth or a lie.

People started to push me away all the more. I got to a place of wanting to shut down, but I knew that God could work this out. So, I continued to press. I would hear preachers speak of how great the Lord is; I knew it for myself, but I still felt trapped. I would say things like, "I feel I am stuck," or "My wheels are spinning in a pit of mud." I would go to a person I thought would understand me and my struggle, but I would get clouded responses that would confuse me more than anything.

The main thing I believe the Lord would have you get from this chapter is an admonition to wait on Him and not get weary. Don't expect man to do what the Lord is seeking to do in your life. In Isaiah 40:31 we are assured that *"they that wait upon the* L ORD *shall renew their strength; they shall mount up with wings as eagles; they shall run, and not be weary; and they shall walk, and not faint."* Your strength can be renewed; the chains of bondage and captivity in which the enemy thinks he has you can be broken. Healing is available through the Lord Jesus Christ. Just don't give in. Endure, for the reward of the

Lord is great. Hold on to your faith and press toward your Lord and Savior Jesus Christ.

In James 4:7-10 we receive these instructions: *"Submit yourselves therefore to God. Resist the devil, and he will flee from you. Draw nigh to God, and he will draw nigh to you. Cleanse your hands, ye sinners; and purify your hearts, ye double minded. Be afflicted, and mourn, and weep: let your laughter be turned to mourning, and your joy to heaviness. Humble yourselves in the sight of the Lord, and he shall lift you up."* As I studied this Scripture, I learned that James is giving us five ways to come near to God.

First, we are being told to submit to God, which means to yield to His authority and will in our lives. We are being instructed to commit our lives to Him and His control and have a willing heart to follow Him. Second, we are instructed to resist the devil. We cannot fall prey to the temptations and traps he sets for us. If someone upsets you, it's easy to get upset and talk about that person, but the best course of action is to pray for him or her. Don't always take the easy way out. Stand for what will challenge your faith and ultimately strengthen you according to the Word of God. Thirdly, we are to wash our hands and purify our hearts. You may have endured hurts in the past, but don't allow them to cripple you. Don't allow them to suffocate you. When we were reborn into the Kingdom of Light, we became new creations. The devil is operating from old information on who you are, but God has rewritten your history in His story! The fourth instruction given is to grieve, mourn, and wail in sincere sorrow. Have a deep desire to be healed and set free. God already knows your motives anyway, so don't be one who is seeking these things only because you got caught in your mess. You must have a sincere desire to be freed from these things that hold you in bondage. The last instruction given by James is to humble yourself before the Lord; when you do, He will lift you up. God is the only One Who has the power and authority to lift you up, so keep your focus on Him. I remember the Lord telling me, "You are focusing on the wrong things. If you continue to focus on those things, you will die spiritually." I felt it happening. I felt that people didn't like me, so I would try my hardest to be nice and do things for them, which just hindered me more.

One day I heard the Lord tell me, "The things you did while you were unsaved you are still doing, even though you are saved." I had to ask the Lord what He meant. I knew that when I was in the world I was fornicating, but when I got saved, that stopped — I began to see the value God had given me and learned that nonmarital sex wasn't pleasing to God. So, what was I still doing? He said, "You changed your behavior, but your motive was the same. You were searching for love and acceptance, and you felt that if you gave yourself to a man, you would eventually receive what you had been searching for. I had your heart at age 12, but you didn't have an understanding of Who I was in your life, so you searched many years to find me again. Now you are in the Body of Christ, still giving yourself away, not fully knowing the value that I have placed on your life. Yes, you are committed to the works of the ministry, but you are still working to receive love and acceptance from man.

"Yes, you love me, and I see that you love my people," God said, "but your hunger and thirst to be loved and accepted is clouding your understanding of what I truly need from you." I had to repent of being a people pleaser in the Body of Christ!

One final comment regarding the desire to receive something you're not getting from people: If you begin to manipulate a situation to receive what you *think* you should be receiving; you have now opened the door to witchcraft entering your life. Anytime you use manipulation to gain what you want; witchcraft is in operation. Therefore, guard your heart with all diligence and allow the Lord to give you what you need. Trust in the Lord for all things, acknowledge Him, and allow Him to order your steps.

I end this chapter by warning you not to allow the devil to hold you captive. God has so much more for you than the devil can ever offer you. We see in Matthew 4:9 that Satan tempts Jesus by saying, *"... All these things will I give thee, if thou wilt fall down and worship me."* Now how crazy is this — the devil offering to Jesus those things that already belong to Him! Don't allow the enemy to steal those things that Jesus has already set aside with your name on it. Stand up and walk in the power that has been given you. Even if you don't *feel* the power, know that it is there working on your behalf.

PRAYER TO OVERCOME CAPTIVITY

Lord, I come to You thanking You for Your son Jesus Christ, who came to set the captives free and give me life – a life more abundant. I am victorious in Christ Jesus. I decree and declare that the devil has no authority over me ... I have power and authority over him! I ask, God, that You cleanse me in every area of my life and that You purify my heart and mind today. I ask You, Lord, to increase me that I may fight my internal battles. I know that man cannot see the full depths of these battles, but my Lord and Savior Jesus Christ knows all and is able to overcome all by the blood He shed on the cross. I submit to your ways, Lord. I confess those things that aren't right in my life, and I turn them over to you right now. In Jesu's Name I pray, Amen!

Conviction

As you become indwelled with the Holy Spirit and align yourself with the Word of God, you will begin to see areas where you fall short in your walk. Don't get disappointed in yourself. The Lord already knows our shortfalls and will forgive us when we repent. In Romans 3:23-26, we learn, *"For all have sinned, and come short of the glory of God; Being justified freely by his grace through the redemption that is in Christ Jesus: Whom God hath set forth to be a propitiation through faith in his blood, to declare his righteousness for the remission of sins that are past, through the forbearance of God; To declare, I say, at this time his righteousness: that he might be just, and the justifier of him which believeth in Jesus."*

The Word of God is the guide we should follow to live our lives according to how the Lord wants us to live. We are created in His image; through the Word we learn who He is, so ultimately, we learn who we are. As we begin to learn who we are, we also learn where we have made mistakes in life in this journey called life. We can't get upset, discouraged, and broken down over what we have done, but we can change what we do. In Romans 3:23, we see that we all fall short. We actually fall short on a daily basis. So many times, verse 23 is quoted, and we move on. But the next verse tells us that we are justified freely through the redemption of Christ, and by His grace. "Justified" means to be declared not guilty. What? I fall short of God's glory through my sins, and then I'm justified and found not guilty? Exactly! Because Christ died for our sins, He took our place so that we might live. Redemption took place — God forgave our sins through the sacrifice of His Son Jesus, and our sin debt was removed from our record. We have been redeemed by the blood of the Lamb and been made righteous.

We must realize that the Word of God is alive today and will "speak" to use in our situations. We can't get upset at ourselves. We must understand that there are two forces always at work: God's desires for us and Satan's desires. One is for us and the other is against us. We have to come to the realization that only God's ways will sustain us, and in order for the Lord to increase in our lives, we must decrease. John the Baptist said as much in Chapter 3, verse 30: *"He must increase, but I must decrease."* This Scripture shows that John the Baptist was in a place of humility, knowing that he was the weaker of the two when it came to him and Jesus. What we must ask God to do is decrease our own flesh so that His spirit can rule. As this process is taking place, our actions will come into alignment with His Word. If you are feeling convicted by things you once did, they are being tried by the Word of God, that's a good thing … it means that the Holy Spirit is on the scene. One of the works of the Holy Spirit is to convict the sin in our lives. This is because we are the temples of the Holy Spirit and He cannot remain where sin also resides. (That's why repentance is so important.)

As mentioned earlier, we were bought with a price … the blood of Jesus. That means we are no longer our own; we belong to God and it is through His Holy Spirit that He resides within us. We now have to examine ourselves and make sure our lives align with the Word, because in John 14:23, we are told by Jesus himself that, *"if a man love me, he will keep my words: and my Father will love him, and we will come unto him, and make our abode with him."* The Holy Spirit is the very essence of Jesus. We were told that the Holy Spirit is our Comforter as well as our guide and gauge, according to John 14:26, *"he shall teach you all things, and bring all things to your remembrance."* The Holy Spirit will warn us when we are veering off into areas the Lord does not desire us to go. He will bring us back by reminding us. Through conviction, He will keep us from doing something that we cannot undo. He will prod our hearts and prick our innermost beings to bring us to a place of confession and repentance. The Holy Spirit comes in a gentle manner to bring us back to a place of right standing; but if His prompting goes unnoticed by us, He will prod more firmly. This prodding can become unpleasant, but it's for our good. God loves us enough to not just leave us alone. He always has our best interests at heart and does not want any harm to come our way. The Holy Spirit is the one who gives us the assurance of our salvation and eternal life.

Allow the Lord to have His way in your life. Allow Him to have controlling interest because He already knows the end result. In Isaiah 46:10, we are told that God is declaring the end from the beginning, which means He already has our lives mapped out completely. I often refer to God's plan for our lives as a movie on a VHS videotape. Our individual moves are already completed in heaven before God placed us in our mother's wombs. It was upon our arrival on earth that the "play" button was hit. Now, we are just living out what He has destined for us. He already knows every mistake we are going to make; they are already factored into our destiny. Just have the mind to decrease yourself so that the Lord will increase within. Be available to serve Him with all that is within you.

Walk in the remission of sins and the forgiveness God gave you more than 2,000 years ago. Be free!

PRAYER FOR CONVICTION

Lord, I ask that You continue to convict my heart and mold me into who You desire me to be. I want You to flow freely and have rule and reign in my life. I trust You, God, because You are my Creator — my manufacturer — and I desire to operate according to the blueprints You have created for me. I know that I am Your child and You love me unconditionally. I know that when I am being convicted in my thoughts and in my spirit, it is only because You want the best for Your child. I pray now that You empower me to yield to Your will and crucify the flesh that threatens to separate us. In Jesus' Name I pray, Amen.

Challenges/Criticism

We are going to be challenged in this Christian journey. We will learn of how God wants His people to operate, but as our spirits are enlightened to God's ways, we must realize that man is still man and we will be posed with challenges. Some of these challenges may make us feel very frustrated. Some may make us want to give up. Some may just completely blow our minds. Know that during our challenges, we are being stretched to expand. It's just like when we work out to tone our bodies — our muscles are stretched and the pain comes. If we endure, the positive results will become evident.

Accept the challenges God places in your path. Do not lower your standards or bow out of your commitment to the Lord. Accept the challenges and handle them according to His leading. Remember to also enjoy life to the fullest, even during the bad times. Understand who you are, and understand that you are valuable to God. God will speak, but you must listen.

What do you do when you hear God, but you don't know what to do? This is a loaded question. If God has told you what to do and you don't do it, you won't feel right because you have not obeyed the Lord. But if you do it, and things don't go the way you expected them to, you will still feel wrong. Before you step out and do *anything*, make sure you have truly heard from the Lord. He will never make you do anything that is contrary to His Word. Also, don't be too quick to run with a word or a revelation. If the Lord gave it to you, He will give you instructions on how to deliver it. Accept the challenge and get the proper instructions. God won't just push you out on a plank; step-by-step instructions will come. In the Old Testament, for instance, He gave the Israelites detailed instructions as to how the tabernacle should be built. He also gave Noah specific instructions on how the ark should be built. So, don't be so quick to act; stay in the presence of the Lord to receive all that is needed. You may understand what is being given to you, but God will enable you to articulate it in a way that others will receive it.

There are two things you need to remember when it comes to a Godly but challenging assignment: First, it's not about you; it's about the Lord and what He wants to give to His people. You are only the vessel being used, so don't add to or take away from what God had given to you. Accept the challenge in its entirety. Second, you cannot allow the reactions of people dictate your actions. Once you master these two keys to meeting a challenge successfully, you are well on your way.

There will be times when you accept a challenge from the Lord, but find that when you step out you are not received. That may be part of God's plan for your growth, so shake off your offense and keep moving. There are some who may not fully understand you, but God completely understands you.

I am reminded of the story of the farmer's donkey. Let's look at the story a little closer:

> *One day a farmer's donkey fell down into a well. The animal cried piteously for hours as the farmer tried to figure out a way to get him out. Finally, he decided it was probably impossible and the animal was old and the well was dry anyway, so it just wasn't worth it to try*

and retrieve the donkey. So, the farmer asked his neighbors to come over and help him cover up the well. They all grabbed shovels and began to shovel dirt into the well.

At first, when the donkey realized what was happening, he cried horribly. Then, to everyone's amazement, he quieted down and let out some happy brays. A few shovel loads later, the farmer looked down the well to see what was happening and was astonished at what he saw. With every shovel of dirt that hit his back, the donkey was shaking it off and taking a step up.

As the farmer's neighbors continued to shovel dirt on top of the animal, he continued to shake it off and take a step up. Pretty soon, to everyone's amazement, the donkey stepped up over the edge of the well and trotted off!

Moral: Life is going to shovel dirt on you. ... Every adversity can be turned into a stepping stone. The way to get out of the deepest well is by never giving up but by shaking yourself off and taking a step up.

What happens to you isn't nearly as important as how you react to it.

This fable tells us that we can't just be reactive when things don't go right. We need to dust ourselves off, take a step up, and keep on moving. Jesus told the disciples this. He said in Matthew 10:14: *"And whosoever shall not receive you, nor hear your words, when ye depart out of that house or city, shake off the dust of your feet."* This is coming from Jesus Himself, so that is what we need to do. We don't have to stew over our rejection and get upset. We can't control others. We can only do what the Lord wants us to do. If people don't receive us, that's for them to deal with, not you.

Trust God in all that you do. Ask Him to order your steps and direct your path. Speak His Word back to Him, because His Word will never return to Him void (Isaiah 55:11). Remember that God is a triune being, so if He is in your life you are always walking in the company of three. You will never be alone when you have the Holy Spirit because He lives on the inside of you. But He is also the Father and the Son. If you are walking in His ways, God will keep you covered. If you jump out of line and decide to not submit to Him, you will be out of order, so there is no guarantee that He will have your back. It's not that He will never forgive you again. But it's important to follow His divine order always. We need the Word to work for us, but if we aren't following it, then its effect becomes null and void in our lives. We can't live in sin and expect God to bless us. Let's look at John 9:31: *"Now we know that God heareth not sinners: but if any man be a worshipper of God, and doeth his will, him he heareth."* We must be in the will of God.

Begin to thank God in all areas of your life. Thank Him for the good, the bad, and the ugly. We have discussed correction previously; praise Him for correction because it's a way of preparing you to meet your next challenge. Praise Him for the criticism and condemnation you may receive. As long as you obeyed God, you made a difference, so praise Him! Seek to learn a lesson in all that you set out to do; if you fail, praise God anyway. Don't get stuck in a place of self-pity, stagnation, or low self-worth. Know that you are valuable to the Kingdom of God and that you are merely experiencing growing pains. Just because you overcame in one area does not mean you have received all the healing and deliverance needed to be whole in Christ Jesus. Please, please, please don't turn back to your old, sinful ways and habits. Don't allow the enemy to dupe you into backsliding into areas out of which you know God has delivered you. In the previous chapter, we discussed how demonic spirits can come back in larger numbers if they find that the house they were once driven from is vacant. Don't allow a demon reinfestation! Stand firm, stand strong, and be immovable, always abounding in the work of the Lord (1 Corinthians 15:58).

Criticism may come, but check the source. If the source is a viable source, one that is nurturing and loving, receive it. If it is coming from one who you know wants to tear you down, rebuke it. Either way, keep on moving! The devil can't catch a moving target. The best way to get caught by the devil is to sit down and sulk about your problems.

We are never going to be perfect, but our job here on the earth is to edify those in our midst and help them to grow in the Lord. The only perfect person to walk this earth was the Lord Jesus Christ Himself. So, accept the Lord's challenge. Put your best out there and do what you can do. Help those around you. Trust that something you say and do will help those you encounter.

One important way God will challenge you is by requiring you to step out of your comfort zone. If Moses had stayed where he was comfortable, he would not have led the children of Israel out of captivity. If he had not been obedient, they would have remained in bondage until God raised up the next person. God always has a backup plan when a chosen servant refuses or fails to fulfill his purpose. It's for various reasons that people fail to fulfill their purpose in life, but the most common reason is fear. Fear will grip people and hinder them from truly walking in what the Lord desires of them. We must "be strong in the Lord" in order to move in what God is telling us to do, even if it takes us into unfamiliar territory. We can't give in to weakness and timidity.

If you make a mistake, that's all right — God is a God of grace and mercy. Man will try to beat you down and make it seem as though you did something awful. But God will allow you to learn from the mistake and keep moving ... which actually brings Him pleasure because you're stepping out in faith, striving to improve, and willing to achieve. So, don't get bogged down by what man is saying. Man is not in control. The Almighty God is in control. Trust God, move in God, lean on God, depend on God; He's the only one on whom you can truly depend. Those who are married depend on their spouses, but sometimes situations arise that cause a loss of trust and, therefore, hinders that dependency. God's dependability is greater even than that of a mother for her child. He's got you like no human can ever have you!

Know that God is the same yesterday, today, and forever. You cannot stay put and you cannot stay rooted in man. Man will say one thing one day and something totally different the next day. If your dependency is in man, you can go crazy.

God *had* a foundation and *is* the foundation. The Bible speaks of Jesus Christ (God the Son) being the Chief Cornerstone. A good foundation is solid and firm. If God is our foundation, it means He is solid and firm. If you have to move the foundation of a house, you have to do some heavy work. You can't move a foundation like you can a roof. The roof is on top of the house, but everything is built upon the foundation! In the spiritual sense, a foundation is what you are built on ... it's your grounding. You must have a stable foundation. That stability comes in God and through God. It comes when you operate through His spirit and refuse to allow the various things not of God – the enemy, man, fear – to come in and infiltrate your mind. You must be firm in your understanding of who you are in God. The enemy will come in and try to kill your dreams, kill your drive, kill your passion, and kill your desire to do those things you know God is telling you to do. Often, he will make these attempts through the criticism of others. He will work through man to get you off focus and miss the blessings God has for you. You can't allow criticism to paralyze you.

The enemy will not only attack through criticism; he will plant doubt and suspicion in your mind to cause you to sever relationships with those who are in your corner. That is why the battle is so tough sometimes. You must operate in God's wisdom because the enemy may be using man against you without them even realizing it. He is a deceiver for sure, so you must stay focused and trust God at all times. You must be firm in your foundation. You have to be firm in your belief and you need to be firm in your understanding of who God is, who Christ is, who the Holy Spirit is and how they operate in your life and the lives of others in the Kingdom. God's benefits are available to every believer — not just the elect few, not just those in fivefold ministry, not just those who have a certificate that identifies them as clergy. It is available to all who confess with their mouth and believe in their hearts that Jesus Christ died on the cross, defeated the devil in hell, rose again, and is now seated at the right hand of the Father.

We must remember to always fight our battles in prayer and on our knees. We can't fight with our mouths or seek revenge in our flesh because we are subject to end up looking no different from our adversaries. Then confusion will come to those who might otherwise have been saved. They'll decide they don't want any part of this "Christian journey." They'll choose to work things out in the world because so many times the world treats them so much better. So, we must have the tenacity to do the right thing. As William J. Toms once said, "Be careful how you live. You may be the only Bible some person ever reads."

That is why dependence on God is so important. If you put your trust in man, you are setting yourself up for failure. Man has up days and down days, but God is the same always. You must have open communication with the Lord and, when something doesn't feel right, seek Him for answers. (I often make the mistake of going to man asking questions when I should just go to the Source.) God will reveal things to you when you commune with Him and seek Him. You can't figure it all out on your own; you have to open the lines of communication with Him. You will be defeated every time if you try to do God's work on your own power. That's not how it works. Just like a lamp needs electricity, we need the Lord! When a lamp is plugged into an electrical socket, the actual source isn't the socket or the electrical wires inside and outside the home. The source — the foundation — is the power plant generating the electricity. You must connect the lamp cord to the socket to tap into the source of the electricity. That's how prayer works. You must seek the source to get the results you need.

Be encouraged and keep pressing on, no matter what your challenges are or how harsh man's criticism may be. Sometimes, you're your own worst enemy. You're constantly trying to figure things out on your own, but you can't. God is standing before you, saying, "Come to me; I have the answers." But your vision is clouded and you don't see Him; the enemy is telling you lies and you believe them. This stubbornness is causing you to go through unnecessary hell because you refuse to seek the Father and are not utilizing the mind of Christ ... which we possess, according to 1 Corinthians 2:16.

We have been given many gifts, but we have to challenge ourselves every day to be overcomers. You must challenge yourself every day to receive the things you need from God and toss out the things Satan sent as weapons of hindrance, distortion and distraction. Learn the lessons you need to learn, and keep moving. Take the lickin' and keep on tickin'. Don't stop, don't quit, don't give up, and don't throw in the towel. According to Ecclesiastics 3, there's a time and a season for all things. There is a time and season to do the good; don't just focus on the bad. Know that there is a time and season to persevere. Be secure in the knowledge that whatever God has for you, you will keep pressing toward so that it can come to pass. Just trust Him. Believe that He is the God of all creation, the King of Kings and the Lord of Lords, the All-Sufficient One. Everything you need is in Him.

PRAYER FOR CHALLENGES AND CRITICISM

Lord, I thank You for the challenges I face in all areas of my life. I realize that these challenges are designed to develop me into the person You desire me to be. They build my strength in You. They root me in my foundation, Christ, and they develop my trust in You. Thank You for the challenges that bring me outside my comfort zone and cause me to further walk in Your grace and Your mercy. Thank You for positive criticism that pushes me to do better; thank You for negative criticism that also allows me to learn lessons and develop spiritually. Thank You for Your Word, available to me at all times. Thank You for always being with me in Your three persons — Father, Son and Holy Spirit. I desire to walk in Your ways and Your character, so I thank You for making Yourself available to me. Help me to pray continually for all mankind, not just those I love. Your Word says we must also pray for those that despitefully use us. That's where our biggest challenge comes, but Father, I step up to the challenge. In Jesus' Name I pray – Amen!

Calling

What is your calling? Or let me put the question this way: What is your personal ministry?

Your personal ministry is the very thing that God has placed in your heart to do ... your calling, so to speak. Every one of us has a distinct personal ministry ... a ministry that does not necessarily involve operating as an apostle, prophet, evangelist, pastor or teacher or being behind a pulpit. You can be part of a church ministry and still walk in a personal ministry, whether it's a ministry of helps (tending to the pastor's needs, cleaning the church, greeting church visitors) or a marketplace ministry (using your business or profession as a base to carry out God's mandates). You don't have to have a title for personal ministry; you just need a heart that is committed to working for the Lord.

But know that when you're walking in your calling, everything is not going to be clean and pretty. Sometimes, you are going to get dirty.

Let's look at the story of Gideon, the Old Testament leader God chose to defeat the Midianites. Gideon had about 32,000 soldiers; he was told to downgrade their number to 10,000. God later had him make the army even smaller. He gave Gideon direction on how to choose those that would go forward with him: have the soldiers go to the water and drink. The 300 men who lapped the water like a dog (as opposed to kneeling to drink) and stayed alert to their surroundings were the ones the Lord chosen for battle. These were the ones God identified as dedicated to the mission to defeat the enemy. They were indeed victorious. They showed that carrying out one's calling isn't a lift of glamor or show. It's a life of being diligent, dependable, and prepared.

Today, the churches are full of those who say they are in God's army. However, there are only a few who will get down and get dirty to complete the work that is before them. What's more, it would seem as though the people who are working their hardest to fulfill the will of God are the ones being persecuted! They often come under criticism for the ways in which they perform their responsibilities.

If you are working hard for the Lord and taking flak for your trouble, I encourage you to lift your head and do your work joyfully and with integrity. This is a challenging thing to do, I know. I have been there. I have been discouraged. I must confess that I struggled a bit, but I continued to fight. Don't allow anything to steal your passion and hinder your personal ministry ... your calling.

God may call multiple people to do the same thing, but they won't all do that same thing in the same manner. Just because you are called to do something does not mean others can't do it, or that your way of doing it is the only way. Don't allow jealousy to keep you from walking in the duties of your personal ministry. Don't let jealousy make you second-guess what God told you to do, or make you think you are doing something wrong. Just know that if God gave *you* a personal ministry along with instructions on how you were to do it, you need to be obedient, no matter what. If people are trying to change your mode of operation, kindly thank them for their recommendation. Seek the Lord and see if their suggestion fits in with how God wants you to carry out your calling. If so, implement the suggestion according to how the Lord instructs; if not, move forward with the way God gave you the assignment. We can't go changing God's instructions just because others can't do what you do.

I have heard people tell me so many times, "I can't do what you do." They are exactly right — they cannot do what I do the way I do it. That's not because what I do is so glamorous or so great or so hard or so difficult. It's because I am a unique individual and God created me to carry out my assignment in a way unique to me. I'm not saying that to be arrogant or prideful; I'm just being honest. I do what I do because God equipped me to do it. You can't do what I do because you are equipped with your own gifts, talents, and skills and God wants you to use those things in a way that's unique to you. People forget that oftentimes. They just want to tag on to what you are doing, but God has given each of us a personal ministry that is like no other.

On the flip side, you can't get upset *because* others aren't able to do what you do. Because we have different callings, our individual capacities will not be the same. It will all balance out. God has ensured that we can work together in unity while completing different tasks and assignments.

In Romans 12:1-2 Paul writes, *"I beseech you therefore, brethren, by the mercies of God, that ye present your bodies a living sacrifice, holy, acceptable unto God, which is your reasonable service. And be not conformed to this world: but be ye transformed by the renewing of your mind, that ye may prove what is that good, and acceptable, and perfect, will of God."* Then in Matthew 16:24, we see what Jesus desired of His recruits: *"... If any man will come after me, let him deny himself, and take up his cross, and follow me."* You see, once we receive Christ Jesus, we are not our own. Jesus died to save our lives. We have been bought with a price, redeemed by the Blood of the Lamb.

The word "sacrifice," according to TheFreeDictionary.com, means to give up something of great value for the sake of something else regarded as more important or worthy. When we are a living sacrifice, we give up our own lives for the benefit of Christ. When you serve the Lord, you make yourself available to Him always. Your main desire is to please and serve Him. (You must be careful because some may see your servant's heart and try to take advantage of you. But as long as you stay connected to the Lord, He will direct your steps.

The Oxford Dictionaries website defines "redeem" as "gain or regain possession of (something) in exchange for payment." Jesus sacrificed His sinless life to take on the sin of the entire world so that we could be reconciled to and reclaimed by the Lord. The Old Testament Book of Genesis shows that God created man in His image: *"And God said, Let us make man in our image, after our likeness: and let them have dominion over the fish of the sea, and over the fowl of the air, and over the cattle, and over all the earth, and over every creeping thing that creepeth upon the earth. So God created man in his own image, in the image of God created he him; male and female created he them."* (Genesis 1:26-27*).* We can see that when Christ gave His life for us, He was redeeming us, or purchasing us back, and returning us to our original place with the Lord. That is why we have victory over the devil.

God's gift of dominion shows me that the Lord already knew that the serpent, Satan, was going to come, wreak havoc, and cause man to fall. So, when the Word says we are redeemed, it means we were returned to our original position with the Lord. We have been forgiven of all and are urged to take up our cross and follow Christ. This means that our ways should become His ways.

When we aren't fully submitted to God or our trials seem too difficult, we may fall. But we shouldn't be discouraged. God already knows our struggles, both intrinsic and extrinsic. Sometimes our struggles have more do with what is on the inside of us then the outside. Outside forces may trigger something that has not yet been dealt with on the inside. The good news is we are the righteousness of God through Jesus Christ, so when we fall, the show is not over.

> ***But now the righteousness of God without the law is manifested, being witnessed by the law and the prophets; Even the righteousness of God which is by faith of Jesus Christ unto all and upon all them that believe: for there is no difference: For all have sinned, and come short of the glory of God; Being justified freely by his grace through the redemption that is in Christ Jesus: Whom God hath set forth to be a propitiation through faith in his blood, to declare his righteousness for the remission of sins that are past, through the forbearance of God; To declare, I say, at this time his righteousness: that he might be just, and the justifier of him which believeth in Jesus. (Romans 3:21-26)***

This New Testament Scripture supports the point made in Proverbs 24:16: *"For a just man falleth seven times, and riseth up again: but the wicked shall fall into mischief."*

Don't allow the enemy to heap coals on you when you make a mistake. Repent, make changes in your life, and continue to walk in your calling. God is all-knowing and all-sufficient, meaning He is forgiving. He's not going to banish you for a mistake; don't let anyone scare you into thinking that. Just as a toddler may fall several times while learning how to walk, so will those coming into the Kingdom and into the knowledge of God.

But we have all heard the saying, "I've fallen and I can't get up." This saying goes back to a commercial for a medical-alert device enabling the elderly to call for help when they injure themselves. No matter what our age, we are all subject to fall spiritually. But, with determination and tenacity within to serve the Lord no matter what, we can get back up and step back into our rightful place in the Lord. Remember that you can do all things through Christ who strengthens you! Don't let a fall hinder you or the calling on your life.

Your calling is very important. Many think of a calling as the fivefold ministry: the apostle, the prophet, the evangelist, the pastor and the teacher. But, above all, we are all called to be servants. Don't get caught up with titles; be caught up in the things that bring the Lord pleasure, glory and honor. Ask Him what His purpose and destiny for you is. It all goes back to the gifts and talents He gave you before you were in your mother's womb. Don't stray from what He has placed within you to be like others. The personal ministry that is your calling will be more pleasing to Him than anything you try to do on your own. God wants you to be submitted to Him because you are a piece in His master plan for all of creation.

PRAYER FOR CALLING

Lord, thank You for creating me. It's my desire to fulfill what You had in mind for me when You placed me in my mother's womb. You saw a need in this earth realm and created me to fulfill that need. Today, Lord, I ask You to show me what You desire me to do. Please reveal the calling on my life so that I can step into Your divine will for my life. It is my desire to serve You and lay down my life for You. I know that losing my life for Your sake means that I gain more of You. Lord, I trust You and know that it is only because of You that I live;

it is only because of You that I move; and it is only because of You that I have my very being. I completely understand that You are my Source. Without You I can do nothing, but with You I know that ALL things are possible. I may fall from time to time, but I know I can get back up and go on to be more effective for You. Have Your way in my life. I decrease myself so that You have more room to fill me up. In Jesus' Name I pray, Amen.

Complacency

Have you ever been in a place where you didn't feel like yourself and were going through the motions? You have dreams and desires, but you also feel that something is holding you back from getting to where you know you are supposed to be. It's not like procrastination. You may feel like you are fighting within, but are just not able to break down what is *happening* within.

I remember when I experienced this feeling of complacency, I remember feeling numb to my surroundings. It almost felt like I stepped outside my life and was watching it from afar and that I had no control or solution to fix it.

Being in this state of complacency is a tactic of the enemy to keep you from living the abundant life that Jesus died for you to have. Complacency silences dreams and smothers passion.

When you are in a place of complacency, confusion may come in and play a factor in your situation. You may begin to question your life based on the feelings deep inside that you are unable to explain or even verbalize.

Let's look at a snippet from Dr. Cindy Trimm's book, *The 40 Day Soul Fast*. On Day Twenty, when she addresses Conquering, she shows how the enemy can confuse us:

> *Don't be naive. You have an enemy who is determined to steal your destiny, kill your heart, and destroy everything you care about. He wants to convince you that you're not worthy of God's love and that you're [incapable] of achieving something great. He doesn't have to eliminate you, but merely control your thoughts. It would be easy to recognize and resist him and his cohorts if they came to you and told you to overtly sin — rob a bank or murder your neighbor. But his favorite ploy is to disguise himself as truth, an angel of light, and invade your thoughts with deceit that is just a little off-center. Then a compounding factor, much like the rate of interest, takes over. The first thought gets built upon another thought; a lie believed gets added to another lie; until finally that single erroneous thought becomes a major controlling pattern in your life. That is what the Scripture calls a stronghold, a place of imprisonment.*

You are a target of the enemy and we all know that he wants to deceive us and kill, steal and destroy all that God has for us. Jesus states the devil's intentions in John 10:10, but He also gives us some blessed assurance at the end of this same verse: *"I am come that they might have life, and that they might have it more abundantly."*

Prayer is the key to knowing what your next steps should be. Prayer is communing with the Father, seeking His ways and listening to His instruction. Let's look at Philippians 4:6-9 to see how Paul admonishes us:

> *Be careful for nothing; but in every thing by prayer and supplication with thanksgiving let*

your requests be made known unto God. And the peace of God, which passeth all understanding, shall keep your hearts and minds through Christ Jesus. Finally, brethren, whatsoever things are true, whatsoever things are honest, whatsoever things are just, whatsoever things are pure, whatsoever things are lovely, whatsoever things are of good report; if there be any virtue, and if there be any praise, think on these things. Those things, which ye have both learned, and received, and heard, and seen in me, do: and the God of peace shall be with you.

This Scripture instructs us to pray and outlines the virtues that deserve our meditation.

Worry, grief, anxiety, hatred, and fear are all attacks on our spirit and our mind as offshoots of confusion. The Lord wants to bestow on us His peace ... peace that passes all understanding, in every circumstance. In John 8:44, Jesus has this to say about the devil: *"... When he speaketh a lie, he speaketh of his own: for he is a liar, and the father of it,"* while 1 Corinthians 14:33 shows that *"... God is not the author of confusion, but of peace, as in all churches of the saints."* When we begin to meditate on the thoughts the enemy plants in our heads, we become vexed and uneasy, which is contrary to the ways of the Lord. When we are thinking on the things of the Lord, peace will be with us. Even when all seems lost, the Lord will grant us peace if we will just keep our thoughts on Him and place our trust in Him. He knows all, and has our best interests at heart.

Philippians 4:6-9 is a favorite Scripture of mine. A related Scripture is Proverbs 4:24: *"Keep thy heart with all diligence;*

for out of it are the issues of life." The heart and the mind are connected. We see that connection in 1 Peter 1:13-16 (AMP):

> *So prepare your minds for action, be completely sober [in spirit — steadfast, self-disciplined, spiritually and morally alert], fix your hope completely on the grace [of God] that is coming to you when Jesus Christ is revealed. [Live] as obedient children [of God]; do not be conformed to the evil desires which governed you in your ignorance [before you knew the requirements and transforming power of the good news regarding salvation]. But like the Holy One who called you, be holy yourselves in all your conduct [be set apart from the world by your godly character and moral courage]; because it is written, "YOU SHALL BE HOLY (set apart), FOR I AM HOLY.*

Our minds and thoughts are vital to our progression in the Kingdom. We cannot allow the enemy to plant seeds that will produce an unwanted harvest. We cannot team up with the enemy and then get upset because things aren't going the way we want them to go! We must recognize the deceit of the enemy, walk in our God-given power and authority, and cast those things out of our lives.

If you find that the enemy has maneuvered you into a state of complacency or confusion that has hindered your walk, just cry out to the Lord and ask Him to fix you. The first step to being healed is realizing there is a problem. Don't be ashamed to call on the Lord. He is already there and He already knows what issues you face.

Don't allow your heart to become calloused. When this happens, you come to a place where you feel no emotion and show no sympathy for others. It's times like these where depression will try to creep in and make you think you are all alone.

I remember an instance in which God gave me a revelation about being alone. It was during one of the times I was feeling what I just described above. He took me to Deuteronomy 31:6 *"Be strong and of a good courage, fear not, nor be afraid of them: for the LORD thy God, he it is that doth go with thee; he will not fail thee, nor forsake thee."*

We are told that God is always with us and He will never leave us. So, in that, I was encouraged. Then God took things a bit further. Let's look at John 14:12-20.

> *Verily, verily, I say unto you, He that believeth on me, the works that I do shall he do also; and greater works than these shall he do; because I go unto my Father. And whatsoever ye shall ask in my name, that will I do, that the Father may be glorified in the Son. If ye shall ask any thing in my name, I will do it. If ye love me, keep my commandments. And I will pray the Father, and he shall give you another Comforter, that he may abide with you for ever; Even the Spirit of truth; whom the world cannot receive, because it seeth him not, neither knoweth him: but ye know him; for he dwelleth with you, and shall be in you. I will not leave you comfortless: I will come to you. Yet a little while, and the world seeth me no more; but ye see me: because I live, ye shall live also. At that day ye shall know that I am in my Father, and ye in me, and I in you.*

Did you see all those promises in the Scriptures? Let's put it all together now. First, the Lord encourages us to be strong; then

He confirms that He will always be with us. Then in John, we are told by Jesus that He is going away, but sending a Comforter to dwell within us and be our comfort. In verse 20, He finishes by reviewing His words, saying that I (Jesus) am in the Father; You (you and me) are in me (Jesus); and I (the Holy Spirit) am in you. See it? We are covered all around, inside and out, so we are never alone. We are always in the company of three – the Father, the Son, the Holy Spirit. Today is your last day of thinking that you are all alone. You just learned through the Word of God that this is not the case; it was just another one of the devil's lies to keep you from being productive in the Kingdom of God.

I once came to a place of confusion over some people I depended on to assist me in ministry. I would get upset because it appeared that these people were ignoring me and pushing me away. What was happening is that old feelings of rejection and abandonment that had surfaced in past situations were surfacing in this one. (When a new situation creeps up on you and causes old, unresolved negative feelings to surface, you're upset about the new situation as well as the old situation of which the devil reminded you. Since you didn't deal with those feelings the last time, you're now fighting two – or more — battles at once.)

We have all heard the comment that confusion is of the enemy, and yes, the enemy was having a field day in my thoughts. I would seek counsel from others, but they seemed to push me away. I began to wonder if it was "tough love." Then I concluded that they didn't love me; that they were just using me for my gifts and talents. Hurt and frustrated, I began to pull back from them. One day, I experienced an outburst of rage. As contrary as this was to the ways of the Lord, it was a turning point. I accepted the fact that something within me was seriously wrong. Those old, familiar feelings had all but taken me over again!

The Lord began to show me that in the past, I would endure a situation for a lengthy period ... then walk away. He said, "Each time you walked away, you had to start over." He told me that this time, I had to stay and press through.

Don't let the Devil cause you to miss out on what is truly yours by suppressing your feelings and believing that if you just don't feel with the situations that cloud your vision from embracing all that God has for you. We have all heard the saying, "out of sight out of mind," but we have to deal with things because otherwise this is a great recipe for the Devil to consume too much of your time, attention, and abilities instead of focusing on the things of God and His purpose for your life.

Let's look again at the Scripture to which I just referred. In 2 Corinthians 12:9-10, Paul tells of the Lord's answer to his request to remove a thorn in his flesh: *"And he said unto me, My grace is sufficient for thee: for my strength is made perfect in weakness. Most gladly therefore will I rather glory in my infirmities, that the power of Christ may rest upon me. Therefore I take pleasure in infirmities, in reproaches, in necessities, in persecutions, in distresses for Christ's sake: for when I am weak, then am I strong."* Paul said that he, because of Christ and His power, can have pleasure in his infirmities and that when he is weak, he can gain strength through Christ.

I couldn't do the "Out of sight, out of mind" pretend game. We quote that saying, but in cases like mine, the devil takes advantage of our belief of it. When a new situation creeps up on you, the devil brings up those old feelings Since you didn't deal with the old feelings at that time, you find yourself fighting two battles (or more) at once. And confusion ensues. This will wear you down and make you want to give up.

But remember what we just learned: The Lord will never leave us nor forsake us. And the Bible tells us that when we are weak, He is strong. He desires to bring us out of that dark place of confusion and into His marvelous light. Keep seeking His face and His Word, and He will do it!

PRAYER TO OVERCOME COMPLACENCY AND CONFUSION

Lord, I confess that I have a sound mind. I confess that I have victory over ever thought and that the enemy will not plant any seeds in my mind that are contrary to Your Word. I give You full access to every thought that enters my mind and ask You, Lord, to examine it for its source. Lord, I declare and decree that I am not double-minded and that I keep my focus on You. I will not submit to the enemy and I cannot serve two masters. Lord, You are my Source. I thank You that when the enemy tries to make me feel that I am all alone, I can confess through Your Word that I am in the company of three at all times. I thank You that You rest, rule and abide within me and direct my steps. I thank You for the abundant life that Your Son died on the cross to give me life, and I thank You for being my strength when I am weak. I am an overcomer. In Jesus' Name I pray, Amen.

Christ Jesus

One day, the Lord had me listening to the book of Romans on the audio Bible while I was riding to work. I got stuck on chapter 5. I listened to it a few times to really understand what it was saying.

I began to realize that it was through one person – Adam – that all of mankind fell *into* sin, but it was also through one person – Christ Jesus — who redeemed us *from* sin. I began to realize that it doesn't matter what we go through during this Christian journey as long as we set our eyes on Jesus. We have to know that He is the ultimate solution. His Word says that He is the Way, the Truth and the Life, so He is the One we need to follow. He is the One with whom we need to abide. He is the answer for all things. He is the One Who will provide. He is the One Who intercedes for us before the Father when we don't know what to say, what to pray or what to do. He is the One through whom grace and mercy are given us daily. We were once sinners under a death sentence, but Christ Jesus came for our benefit.

In Christ Jesus, we are more than conquerors. Any time we face an issue, whether or not it was discussed in this book, we can take it to Christ Jesus and He will have our solution. It may not come immediately. But trust and believe in Him, and He will provide it. We can praise Him in the good, the bad and the ugly because He makes us victorious over all things.

When you hear the Lord tell you to do something, be obedient. He speaks with purpose all the time, so when you hear Him, listen carefully for instructions. Allow your spirit to be open to His command. There is a reason for everything the Lord does; He doesn't do anything uncalculated. The enemy will set out to mimic what God does, but the spirit of God cannot be replicated! We have to know the difference. God's spirit is life-breathing. We have the Zoë (divine, eternal) life of God that lives on the inside of us. This Zoë life is the very essence of God Himself, given to us through the Holy Spirit Who dwells within us. God is a triune being and all three persons of the Godhead are all interconnected for our benefit. God sent His Son, Jesus, to set us free from sin. Then, when Jesus ascended into heaven, He sent the Holy Spirit back to live within us, guiding us through the pathways of life and empowering us. (Don't we serve an awesome God?)

We must keep our eyes focused on Christ Jesus. He is the Savior; He is the One Who will get you through every valley; He is the One Who will be with you at every mountain top; He is the One Who will get you through that valley of the shadow of death; He is the One Who will encourage you when you don't feel like being encouraged; He is the One Who is with you always. Christ Jesus is the answer to all things. So, we really don't even have to worry about problems! To save us, God had to send Someone Who was going to do it the right way; Someone Who already knew the end result; Someone Who had to be an example of hope. God had to send Someone Who He knew wouldn't fail in such a critical assignment, one that would enable mankind throughout the generations to be saved, healed and delivered from the tricks, tactics and deception that the enemy.

God's adversary wants to stop the work of the Lord in this earth realm. Satan knows of the goodness established in heaven, but because he wanted God's glory for himself, he was cast out of heaven. The enemy has made it his mission to hinder God's plan, so he uses his deception to taint the walk of those confessing Christ Jesus and walking in the righteousness of God. The devil tries to mock God by using the people confessing God. He started with Adam and Eve in the Garden of Eden, destroying their perfect relationship with the Lord. They were provided all they needed and only given one command: Do not eat from the Tree of Good and Evil. That one command was the same command the enemy twisted around and used to deceive.

I was once shown that the Father, the Son and the Holy Spirit were having a conversation. It's like God was having a meeting with his posse ...which, in reality, was with Himself, since they are all three in one. The three members of the Godhead began to discuss some needs occurring in the earth that needed to be addressed. The solution was to create YOU and supply you with the gifts and talents you needed in order for you to operate in ministry. They were all three present when you were created and birthed.

We may think we have problems, but we have to look at them from a bigger viewpoint — we are a solution to a problem or a situation or a need. Every one of us is a solution to a need God saw on this earth. It doesn't have to be a negative thing. We are a solution, just as Christ Jesus was a solution. God said, "Let me fill this vessel up with this mindset, this gift, this talent, this amount of endurance and determination." He knew that we would face trials. But He also knew that we would be victorious if we followed His master plan as beneficiaries of the sacrifice of His Son, Christ Jesus. "The blood of My Son is available to cover them through every adversity," God said of us. "The precious blood of My Son — who willingly came to earth to die for all of mankind so that they may live — is available to every vessel. He chose to be the sin offering, the sacrificial Lamb."

In the Old Testament, the priests were to bring a lamb as a sin offering, but God realized that He needed a permanent fix to a situation that had been tainted by the enemy. God decided to send His Son to be the Lamb instead. God was determined to deliver His people out of bondage. Jesus already knew the ways of the Father and was already of the Father, so He was the perfect person to fulfill this assignment. Not only did Jesus already know the ways of the Father; the Father knew that Jesus would not compromise and fall short in His assignment. He knew the strength that was in Jesus because He and Jesus were already one. He knew that Jesus would not and could not be manipulated; no matter what, He would do what He needed to do. God knew that the integrity of His sinless Son would be displayed on earth. He knew Jesus would be an example and encourager, letting people know that they can do all things because He makes all things possible.

Just know that Jesus is the Source of freedom and peace. Put your trust in Him — He reigns today!

MY PRAYER TO CHRIST JESUS

Lord, I thank You for You, I thank You for Your Son Jesus, and I thank You for Your Holy Spirit. I know that I need each of You every day of my life — morning, noon and night. I thank You that You sent the Christ, the Anointed One, to come and die for me. He was Your Word that became flesh so that I may live. I thank You for His intercession on my behalf to assist me in this life journey. I have come to realize that He is an asset that I cannot afford to live without. He is my solution to every situation and He is one Who possesses a great love for me. He loved me so much that He chose to die for me.

Lord, continue to keep me covered in this Christian journey. As I begin to face the things discussed in this book, please give me confidence in knowing that You will ALWAYS be with me in every situation. Allow me to learn Your ways so that I may carry out my purpose before Your Son returns to this earth. Allow me to live a consecrated life that will cause me to do away with many of the bad habits I possess, and bring You pleasure. Help me to decrease so that You can increase within me. Help me to be pleasing in Your sight. Help me to repent of any wrong that surfaces in my life. Enable me to walk in obedience and truth at all times, and make it known to me when I have veered from Your plan for my life. In Jesus' Name I pray, Amen.

Message from the Author

Many chapters in this book were extremely difficult to write. One chapter I wrote had to be rewritten because I had to seek the Lord further. That particular chapter was birthed out of hurt and pain, which spewed through the initial words that were written. When I went to God, He showed me where adjustments needed to be made ... not just in the words on the page, but within the things that consumed my heart and mind as well as within my eyes and ears. These areas are all interconnected. If we aren't careful and prayerful, the things we see, hear, and think about will end up hindering us.

There were many times while writing this book that I would go to church and cry my eyes out, but then was able to come home and write what the Lord had shared with me. He would either tell me to go back and write from a different perspective, or He would download a revelation that would help me to understand what He wanted to share within these chapters.

It's important that as we walk and grow, we learn God's way of doing things. You must allow the Lord to heal you completely before stepping out to do certain things. If you step out without being properly suited or in the right mind frame, you will have many setbacks. But know that if you believe in the Lord and are seeking to walk His path, He will be there. You can't walk this Christian journey and have ulterior motives contrary to the will of God. If that is the case, He will not be with you.

The Lord has more than enough blessings ready and waiting for every one of His children. So, endure to the end and trust in Him every step of the way. Remember, we are all children of a king ... not just any king, but the King of Kings and the Lord of Lords. Walk in your victory today!

It is my sincere prayer that the topics discussed in this book have helped you in your Christian journey.

Bibliography

Sneed, Troy. "Lay It Down." *All Is Well*. Emtro Gospel, 2012. CD.

Munizzi, Martha. "Great Exchange." *The Best is Yet to Come*. Integrity Music, 2003. CD.

Trimm, N. Cindy. "Day Twenty: Conquering, Characteristic 20: Order." *The 40 Day Soul Fast: Your Journey to Authentic Living*. Destiny Image Publishers, Inc., 2011. [193]. Print.

Unknown Author. "The Farmer's Donkey: A Fable for Our Time." www.naute.com/stories/donkey.phtml.

Other Publications

ISBN 978-0998026251

When Grace & Mercy Met Me God Cares

A special look at traditional Bible stories and shares from the perspective of the character from the Bible. As the characters came alive in a different way.

We all fail from time to time and God is right there to share His Grace and Mercy with us. Don't beat yourself up for times when you fail, but learn from the lesson and move forward into purpose.

The Adventures of Tricia and the Twelve Paw Crew

978-1735362007   978-1735362045

www.kingdomnewstoday.com

www.ingramcontent.com/pod-product-compliance
Lightning Source LLC
Chambersburg PA
CBHW070949080526
44587CB00015B/2249